$martEssentials®

for

COLLEGE
RENTALS

More Titles In Best-Selling SMART ESSENTIALS® Series

💬 **SMART ESSENTIALS® FOR SELLING YOUR HOME**
How To Get The Highest Price In The Shortest Time

💬 **SMART ESSENTIALS® FOR BUYING A HOME**
How To Get The Best Price And The Lowest Payment

💬 **SMART ESSENTIALS® FOR REAL ESTATE INVESTING**
How To Build Wealth In Rental Property Today

💬 **SMART ESSENTIALS® FOR BUYING FORECLOSURES**
Finding Hidden Bargains For Home Or Profit

💬 **SMART ESSENTIALS® FOR COLLEGE RENTALS**
Parent And Investor Guide To Buying College-Town Real Estate

$martEssentials®
for COLLEGE RENTALS

Parent And Investor Guide To Buying College-Town Real Estate

Dan Gooder Richard

Inkspiration Media

SMART ESSENTIALS® FOR COLLEGE RENTALS
Parent And Investor Guide To Buying College-Town Real Estate

Published by
Inkspiration Media
2724 Dorr Avenue, Suite 103, Fairfax, VA 22031
http://www.SmartEssentials.com

ISTC: A0320120000B4799
Library of Congress Control Number: 2012923088

Publisher's Cataloging-In-Publication Data
(Prepared by The Donohue Group, Inc.)

Richard, Dan Gooder, 1947 –
   Smart Essentials for college rentals: parent and investor guide to
buying college-town real estate / Dan Gooder Richard.
     p. ; cm. — (Smart Essentials series)
   ISBN-13: 978-1-939319-04-3
   ISBN-10: 1-939319-04-8
   1. Real estate investment — United States. 2. Student housing —
United States. 3. Rental housing — United States. 4. Residential real
estate — Purchasing — United States. I. Title. II. Title: College rentals
HD259 .R53 2013
643/.12/0973   2012923088

CONTENTS

CHAPTER 1 :: ORIENTATION 1
- ▶ Make Demographic Trends Your Friend With College Real Estate
- ▶ Discover 5 Top Ways Smart Investors Make Money With Off-Campus Housing
- ▶ Assemble An Advisor Team That Makes Sure You Avoid Costly Mistakes

CHAPTER 2 :: COLLEGE TOWNS 101 15
- ▶ Select The Right College-Town Market For Investment
- ▶ Use Demarcation Zones (DMZs) To Evaluate Locations And Avoid Killer Competition From On-Campus Housing And Apartment Communities
- ▶ Avoid 6 Costly Mistakes Buying In The Wrong College Market

CHAPTER 3 :: GOLDMINES 25
- ▶ Recognize Locations That Produce Profitable Student Rentals Today
- ▶ Find College-Town Properties That Are Worth Buying
- ▶ Avoid All-Too-Common Property Picking Mistakes That Cost Serious Money

CHAPTER 4 :: COLLEGE MATH 35
- ▶ Target A Strategy That Works For You—And Stick To It
- ▶ Separate Profitable Rentals From Money Pits With Surefire Analysis Techniques
- ▶ Negotiate Contract Contingencies To Craft Win-Win Purchase Offers

CHAPTER 5 :: FINANCIAL AID 51
- ▶ Find The Cash You Need To Be A Player In College-Rental Investments
- ▶ Discover Inside Tips To Buy With 'Other People's Money'
- ▶ Pick The Investor Financing Strategy That Fits Your Needs Like A Golden Glove

CHAPTER 6 :: LANDLORD U 61
- ▶ Master The Student-Housing Calendar To Your Advantage
- ▶ Avoid All-Too-Common Housing Discrimination Mistakes
- ▶ Know Everything You Need To Manage Student Rentals

CHAPTER 7 :: GRADUATION 75
- ▶ Time The Right Moment To Cash Out Your Investment
- ▶ Use Equity Buildup To Trigger Your Profit-Taking Strategies
- ▶ Select From Five Ways To Cash Out That Fit Your Investment Goals

About The Series 87

About The Team 89

Smarties' Creed 90

More Titles In Best-Selling SMART ESSENTIALS Series ... 90

CHAPTER 1
ORIENTATION

In this chapter, you'll learn smart ways to:

1. Make demographic trends your friend with college real estate.

2. Discover 5 top ways smart investors make money with off-campus housing.

3. Assemble an advisor team that makes sure you avoid costly mistakes.

DEMOGRAPHICS DRIVE COLLEGE-RENTAL DEMAND

Sending your money to college may be the closest thing to a sure bet in investment real estate these days. It comes down to supply and demand.

Student enrollments in colleges and universities are projected to continuously expand through 2023 and beyond, thanks to the Echo Boomers—children of the Baby Boomers ("Gen Y," "Millennials," "Net Generation") born 1982–1995. Besides waves of Echo Boomers, other students priced out of private universities are headed to public schools. Nontraditional students are swelling the rolls too with returning war veterans on the GI Bill and mid-career types who lost jobs and are looking for retraining.

To serve the expanding student body, growing numbers of faculty, administrators and their families live in college towns. Adding to the gravitational pull from enrollments and staff, there is also an expanding constellation of research, technology and service industries centered in college towns. Also driving demand for more college-town rentals is an ever-growing, asset-rich retiree and alumni base.

The numbers are dramatic. More high school graduates are going to college than ever before. Check out the numbers from the National Center for Education Statistics (NCES), "Projections of Education Statistics to 2020."

Between 2009 and 2020, an 11-year period, projected enrollment increases are as follows:

- ► 13% increase (to 23 million) for total enrollment in postsecondary degree-granting institutions.
- ► 9% increase for students 18 to 24 years old; 21% for students 25 to 34 years old; 16% for students 35 years old and over.
- ► 11% increase for full-time students; 16% for part-time students.
- ► 12% increase for undergraduate students; 18% for post-baccalaureate students.
- ► 13% increase in public institutions; 13% increase in private institutions.
- ► Freshmen fall enrollment will increase from 3.2 million in 2009 to 3.6 million in 2020.

◆ ◆ ◆

Essential Takeaway: *Millions of students will need to rent housing near colleges and universities for many years to come. That demand also allows investors to increase rents over time. Higher rents translate into higher property values when it's time to cash out.*

◆ ◆ ◆

No Rooms At The U

Beyond rising enrollments, a host of other reasons have converged to create a shortage of student housing.

● **Recession budgets.** Cash-strapped state budgets faced with demands for healthcare, infrastructure improvements, and higher education have throttled on-campus housing development to near zero. Why? Dealing with belt-tightening, public university planners realize they can make more from classroom space than they can from housing space.

● **Old dorms.** At many schools, old, obsolete dorms built in the last century drive students to live off-campus. It's a double whammy: (1) Academic and athletic capital projects get higher priority than aging structures needing rehab; (2) Today's wired students demand state-of-the-art amenities and electronic capabilities.

End result? College students are turning to off-campus housing in droves. A shortage of good-quality, close-in housing in most college towns has created the perfect opportunity for smart investors and parents.

● **Parental demand.** Buying student housing[††] property in a college town can be an even better proposition if you have a son or daughter in the area who you shoulder housing expenses for. The $7,000 to $15,000 per year you would pay the college or a landlord for rent could be used to make payments on an investment property. Add to that, the additional rents from several other students living in your investment could turn it into a real money-saver—if not an outright money-maker.

> [††] **Student Housing**
> Student housing refers to both on-campus and off-campus living facilities. Where the institution manages the on-campus "dorms," investment owners manage off-campus rental property. Rental property, particularly multi-unit properties, are officially considered student housing by Fannie Mae (which sets standards for conventional mortgages) when 80% or more of the units are rented to students.

Word To Parents: Why Pay Another Landlord's Mortgage?

Have you ever added up how much in dorm costs or rent you will pay while your kid is in college? Sticker shock! Here are the monthly rent-payment numbers projected for years until graduation. Double or triple the figures for a second or third child in school at the same time:

$350 Rent Per Month:
$8,400 (2 yrs); $12,600 (3 yrs); $16,800 (4 yrs); $21,000 (5 yrs); $25,200 (6 yrs).

$400 Rent Per Month:
$9,600 (2 yrs); $14,400 (3 yrs); $19,200 (4 yrs); $24,000 (5 yrs); $28,800 (6 yrs).

$450 Rent Per Month:
$10,800 (2 yrs); $16,200 (3 yrs); $21,600 (4 yrs); $27,000 (5 yrs); $32,400 (6 yrs).

$500 Rent Per Month:
$12,000 (2 yrs); $18,000 (3 yrs); $24,000 (4 yrs); $30,000 (5 yrs); $36,000 (6 yrs).

$550 Rent Per Month:
$13,200 (2 yrs); $19,800 (3 yrs); $26,400 (4 yrs); $33,000 (5 yrs); $39,600 (6 yrs).

$600 Rent Per Month:
$14,400 (2 yrs); $21,600 (3 yrs); $28,800 (4 yrs); $36,000 (5 yrs); $43,200 (6 yrs).

TOP 10 REASONS COLLEGE REAL ESTATE IS SMART FOR PARENTS

Here are 10 reasons why parents should give owning student housing the "ole college try":

1. Save a bundle (thousands) in housing expenses by bypassing costly university room rates or rent payments to another landlord. (You can also free your child and your pocketbook from high-cost college-sponsored meal plans.)

2. Establish in-state residency (for public institutions) with owner-occupied property and save thousands more with lower in-state tuition rates. A rental property where the investor's student offspring lives is considered "owner occupied" if the offspring is included on deed and/or mortgage.

3. Sell the rental property after college for a profit or keep for siblings to use or as ongoing investment rental.

4. Let other students pay your mortgage and expenses by renting out extra bedrooms and generate rental income greater than received from a whole-property standard lease.

5. Purchase a rental with all cash or a low-down-payment FHA loan with a lower owner-occupied interest rate and minimize monthly payments.

6. Employ a property manager for hands-free management or build your scholar's responsibility and credit before graduation.

7. Minimize vacancies by renting to a never-ending stream of need-to-be-local tenants from undergraduates and graduate students to faculty or university staff.

8. Provide your scholar with a stable, clean, safe and well-maintained living environment during and maybe even after college.

9. Take investor tax breaks as the mortgage holder cum owner who pays the expenses, plus avoid capital gains upon sale because property is your scholar's primary residence.

10. Parents benefit from tenants whose ability to pay is not tied to having jobs, like in the real world. Once your student is through living in your rental, it can become a cash-income source for retirement while offering long-term capital appreciation.

CHAPTER 1

ORIENTATION

◆ ◆ ◆

*Essential Takeaway: Boil down all the supply and demand numbers and there is one college real estate success indicator above all others: **A high percentage of students living off campus.** When the shortage of on-campus housing pushes 70% or more of students to live off campus, occupancy rates go up, rents go up, properties appreciate. Find a school that combines high off-campus living with growing enrollment and the next decade is ready-made for you to invest in college real estate.*

◆ ◆ ◆

5 REASONS COLLEGE REAL ESTATE IS SMART FOR INVESTORS

With a relatively modest amount of capital and income, you can profit from real estate investing — once you recognize the chief elements of the rental-property marketplace (more details in a moment).

If you've bought your own home, you already know many of the financial advantages — and disadvantages — of real estate ownership. Here's a brief overview of the 5 essential ways your modest amount of capital and income can yield a profit when invested in rental real estate today.

1. Lower Your Taxes

If rents break even with expenses or you can tolerate feeding a property with cash, a range of tax deductions can turn a property with negative pretax cash flow into a shelter for other income. Deductions include expenses from interest to insurance and from maintenance to the Big Kahuna: Depreciation.[††] Almost every dollar you spend on your investment property is tax deductible within certain limits. (It is not uncommon, however, that even with a positive-cash-flow property a temporary negative cash flow can be caused by a tenant vacancy or major repair or upgrade.)

CHAPTER 1

ORIENTATION

Two important exceptions to the "everything is deductible" rule:
(1) The portion of your monthly payment that goes toward reducing
your loan balance ("principal payment"); (2) Cash outlays for capital
improvements to the property that must be depreciated. Also, when you
later sell the investment property, some or all the profits you realize may
qualify as long-term capital gains that are taxed at a much lower rate
than ordinary income.

Everything You Need To Know About Depreciation

Beyond the tax deductions allowed for
operating expenses and property taxes, a huge
advantage for investors can be summed up
in one word: Depreciation. The depreciation
deduction alone can sometimes turn a losing
property into a winner.

✝ Depreciation

Depreciation is unquestionably the most important tax
incentive for investment properties. Simply, Uncle Sam
assumes that a building and improvements wear out over time
and become worthless. But land never wears out. That's why
it's essential to know that the land's value must be subtracted
from the sale price to establish your "depreciable base" for tax
purposes. Depreciation "losses" are deductible from income
when, in fact, the property may be increasing in value.
Accountants call depreciation the "write-off for obsolescence."

Rabbit Or Tortoise: Which Depreciation Is Best?

You'll need to decide which of two
depreciation methods is ideal for your
situation: straight-line depreciation or
accelerated depreciation. Sheltering outside
income or producing positive cash flow
are two criteria that will help you decide.

If your tax advisor calls and says, "You've got a problem. Your property
is producing taxable income," that's a nice problem to have. Maybe it's
time to buy another property or two to increase your depreciation
deduction and shelter the income. *Smart Tip:* Get professional tax help.
Tax laws change constantly and today's rules are mind boggling in their
complexity. There's simply no substitute for sound advice from a tax
expert familiar with your situation.

Caution: Assume you benefit from some depreciation deductions, but not enough to turn a negative cash flow positive, at least from a tax viewpoint. Remember: Those depreciation deductions are actually a tax deferral, not a tax exemption. If you hold the property long enough to take excess depreciation beyond the allowed accelerated or straight-line amount, Uncle Sam will "recapture" excess depreciation at sale. Ask your tax advisor to run the numbers for your situation.

2. Pocket Positive Cash Flow

The positive cash-flow strategy is particularly attractive to investors with a goal of lifetime income and with down-payment cash ("equity") to invest from savings, outside income or surplus income from other rental properties. In today's college market, the convergence of lower prices, low interest rates and high rental demand can make the cash-flow strategy a winner.

Quite simply, positive cash flow is having more rent coming in than you pay out in expenses. Cash flow before tax is the difference between income (rents) and expenses (loan payments and operating costs). Subtract expenses from income and if you have money left over, that's positive cash flow. If you have to "feed" the property meter — put money from your pocket toward paying the expenses — you have negative cash flow.

Before or after taxes? Smart college-town investors know that depreciation can turn a negative cash flow *before* taxes into a positive cash flow *after* taxes. The ideal situation for most investors is to have positive cash flow before taxes. How? (1) Make a large down payment that keeps mortgage payments below rental revenue. (2) Hold the property long enough for rents to increase, surpassing expenses. (3) Rehab or expand the property to command a higher rent. Often investors with a need for cash — or parents paying college tuition or living expenses — find pre-tax positive cash flow a smart strategy to produce current income.

3. Use Leverage

The essential rule of leveraging is to use financing ("other people's money" or OPM) as much as possible, and as little of your own cash as possible. By reducing your down payment and increasing financing, leverage[††] lets you control a large investment with a relatively small amount of capital and income.

Not only do you reduce your down payment and closing costs, you also increase your tax deductions through higher mortgage interest payments.

> ††*Leverage*
>
> Leverage is defined as using borrowed money ("non-equity capital") to increase returns on equity. High leverage means a small down payment, and low leverage means a large down payment. Put another way, the highest leverage possible is nothing down. The lowest leverage possible is an all-cash purchase.

How much leverage is just right? The straight answer is: It depends on your investment strategy. A small down payment means higher monthly payments on a larger loan. If you're in a high tax bracket, the higher interest deductions can be an advantage. On the other hand, a large down payment — or paying all cash — means lower or no loan payments, which in turn can give you higher income beyond expenses ("positive cash flow"). If income is your strategy or if your kid lives there rent-free, higher cash up front and lower leverage pays off.

4. Benefit From Appreciation

We've all heard the investment mantra before: Buy low, sell high. Appreciation is the principle behind this wealth builder as the property increases in value over time. In simple terms, profit is appreciation minus expenses. While depreciation reduces taxes, appreciation is how real estate increases in value . . . and ultimately beats inflation.

No one can predict if properties in your college market generally — or your property specifically — will increase or decrease in value. Yet one stunning fact is clear: Throughout the valuation cycles of the last century, there are times when market corrections reset values much lower. Think the Great Depression of the 1930s and the Great Recession of the 2000s. Today's experienced investors know that the period just after a reset offers some of the best opportunities to buy low . . . then hold and sell high later when natural demand and inflation eventually push values up again.

Smart college-town investors know inflation and appreciation won't make you rich quickly. But appreciation *can* make you rich slowly.

If you don't want to wait for prices to escalate, consider another strategy. Renovate the property in a way that minimizes expenses and maximizes your ability to charge higher rents. Smart renovations can create price appreciation beyond inflation.

5. Cash Out Equity Buildup

Last but not least, equity buildup — the difference between the property's value and the outstanding loan balance — is the fifth way to profit from college real estate. As we saw in #4, appreciation is one way your equity grows. Also improvements ("sweat equity") may increase your equity. Another way to riches is through mortgage principal payoff. In a nutshell, renters pay your mortgage every month — another example of using OPM to build wealth.

Some investors call equity buildup "shadow income" because it is not realized until the investor takes the profit through refinancing or selling. The combination of appreciation *and* principal pay-down allows you to set an "equity target" when it's time to cash out. Smart ways to cash out on your equity are detailed in GRADUATION (Chapter 7).

◆ ◆ ◆

Essential Takeaway

Essential Takeaway: Here's how college-town real estate investors get rich slowly: Use only 20% of your money combined with 80% financing (or your 25% with 75% OPM) to buy a property. The investment costs you 20% but entitles you to 100% of the rents. Over time, use the rents to pay down the loan balance. When you sell, that loan pay-down ("equity buildup") increases your investment return (and net worth). Possible price appreciation is icing on a smart investor's cake. Now you know how smart investors and parents get rich slowly with college real estate.

◆ ◆ ◆

As the humorist R.H. Shay is credited with saying, "Depend on the rabbit's foot if you will, but remember it didn't work for the rabbit."

Every market, every property is different. The trick is knowing where to look — and avoiding the pitfalls that lurk in your path. Coming up: Spotting the right location in COLLEGE TOWNS 101 (Chapter 2) and finding the right properties that can produce college-town GOLDMINES (Chapter 3).

RULES OF ENGAGEMENT FOR YOUR TEAM OF 8 ESSENTIAL ADVISORS

No matter if you are interested in single-family homes or small residential properties of one to four units, you'll need a network of pros. Nobody can — or should — do it all by themself.

Why? Buying investment property comes with complexities far beyond those you may have encountered purchasing your own home. Distressed and foreclosed homes present even more pitfalls that can cost you serious money. Quite simply: You need an advisory team.

1. Investor's real estate agent. Successful investing starts with a top real estate professional who specializes in local rental property and investors. These pros see more deals in a month in their local market, than individual investors see in a lifetime. A really good investor agent can help with:

▶ Market data and research
▶ Rental rates
▶ Foreclosure market knowledge
▶ Property search
▶ Negotiation and representation
▶ Financing
▶ Property management
▶ Home repair/cleaning service referrals
▶ Tenant search
▶ Valuation of property
▶ Marketing for sale

When who represents you matters most, experience counts. Look for a top-notch real estate agent who has worked with investors, who knows how to craft a "win-win" purchase offer that a seller will accept and holds advanced certifications such as Certified Commercial Investment Manager (CCIM), Certified Realty Investment Associate

(CRIA) and may also be a certified buyer's agent such as an Accredited Buyer Representative (ABR), or Certified Buyer Representative (CBR). A great agent will know from experience exactly how the local process works and can advise you each step of the way.

The best investor-specialist agents also bring their own network of professional contacts from property managers, tax advisors and appraisers, to lawyers, building inspectors and craftsmen. Your agent's connections are essential, especially if your other advisors don't specialize in real estate or you don't already have a working relationship with the needed local professionals.

Smart Tip: Most professional service expenses are tax deductible when you buy investment property.

◆ ◆ ◆

Essential Takeaway: *The experience of a top real estate agent costs property buyers nothing—property sellers usually pay their commission. Remember, real estate agents don't get paid until a deal closes. That alone is a motivation that works in the investor's interest. Also, top agents value a lifetime association far more than a single transaction. They want you to call them to list a property for sale later on, not just help you buy it at the start. Top agents get most of their business from satisfied referrals. They go the extra mile to earn your continued confidence.*

◆ ◆ ◆

2. **Accountant or tax advisor.** Ignorance of tax laws is understandable—but costly. You'll want a professional in your corner who can advise you about:

▶ Setting up a Limited Liability Corporation (LLC)

▶ Protecting personal assets should someone be injured on your property

▶ Selecting the best depreciation method

▶ Weighing the impact of various deductions

▶ Advising on the best time to sell or refinance—and the tax consequences.

▶ Keeping the books, generating profit-and-loss reports and preparing your tax return.

▶ Tracking how buying investment property affects your overall financial situation.

Your accountant/tax advisor will know about alternative minimum taxes, estate taxes, reallocation of income, imputed interest, limitations on deductions, penalties and more.

3. Lender. Smart investors know that financing ("leverage") can make or break a deal. Plus, the right financing can make an enormous difference in the value and return on your investment. For parents who only plan to buy one property, a residential loan lender will be fine if you don't plan to pay all-cash. For a multi-property investor or investor in multi-family apartment buildings or communities, a supportive commercial mortgage lender is essential.

National banks may offer the best rates and terms and have regulatory requirements to loan locally. Local banks or neighborhood credit unions get to know you and may be most responsive to financing your purchases. Bottom line: Cultivate several good lenders. *Smart Tip:* Lenders have real estate connections. Often they are first to hear of properties that are about to hit the market. Again, if you intend to pay all cash or use "hard money" from a funding source like a partnership, then a supportive lender may not be essential.

4. Property manager. Your most extensive relationship will be with your property manager. Besides being your eyes and ears on the property, one of the greatest values a local property manager brings to you is their network of local contacts. Leasing and managing college-town property can be time-intensive and requires dealing with a lengthy list of people from online and classified operators, prospective renters, utility companies, plumbers, carpenters, electricians, painters, pest inspectors, lawn services, housekeeping companies, even accountants, lenders and attorneys. Much more on property management in Chapter 6: LANDLORD U.

5. Attorney. You'll need a landlord-tenant lawyer for reviewing documents and contracts, checking local zoning or other laws such as rent control and tenant/landlord rights, preparing settlement documents, approving leases and guiding you (heaven forbid) through the eviction process or a tenant lawsuit. The right attorney will be a resource of information and a sounding board for many other decisions.

6. **Inspectors.** The best income properties get scooped up fast, especially foreclosures, which means you must be prepared to move quickly. The trick is to avoid unseen defects that cost thousands to rehab. You'll need a general home inspector to check structure and all systems, plus evidence of fire or water damage, erosion, dry rot, etc. You also may want specialists to inspect as needed for mold, radon, wood-destroying pests, asbestos, lead paint, polybutylene pipes (if property built before 1978), formaldehyde, carbon monoxide, septic, well or water quality, maybe an energy audit or indoor air quality audit, and any local peculiarity, such as clay soil shifting, earthquake risk, landslide/mudslide/rockslide area, toxic waste or record of past violations.

7. **General contractor.** Though you may want to get multiple contractors' estimates later, at least you should have one general contractor at the ready to give you cost estimates for any repairs or improvements that must be made to a property before you can rent it or re-rent it after a tenant moves out. Essentially, your contractor can set a budget that separates the fixer-uppers from the money pits. Hidden rehab costs that surface after you've bought the place are a costly bummer.

8. **Mentor.** A mentor who has been around the track before you can be invaluable. We're not talking an Internet fix-and-flip guru selling seminars and riches beyond your wildest dreams—all for a fat check from you. Rather, find an experienced local investor who gets it. Look for someone you can show your property cash-flow analysis to before you make an offer; someone to answer questions one-on-one; someone who has walked the walk not just talks the talk. If you're a rookie, consider a mentor with cash for whom you do the legwork finding deals in return for experience without the risk. Local investment clubs, landlord associations and your top agent are good resources for finding a mentor.

If you can see yourself in this smart company, then college-town real estate investing could be for you. Go to the head of the class in the next chapter: COLLEGE TOWNS 101.

Chapter 1 Roundup

Smart Essentials ORIENTATION ::
What You Have Learned

▶▶ Demographics drive college rentals demand for decades.

▶▶ Why there are no rooms at the U.

▶▶ Top 10 reasons college real estate is smart for parents.

▶▶ 5 reasons college real estate is smart for investors.

▶▶ Rules of engagement for your team of 8 essential advisors.

COLLEGE TOWNS 101

In this chapter, you'll learn smart ways to:

1. **Select the right college-town market for investment.**

2. **Use Demarcation Zones (DMZs) to evaluate locations and avoid killer competition from on-campus housing and apartment communities.**

3. **Avoid 6 costly mistakes buying in the wrong college market.**

HOW TO SPOT A GOOD COLLEGE-TOWN MARKET

Market? Location? Property? Let's cut to the chase. Above all, student-housing investors require a steady stream of available tenants. One rule of thumb is to divide the number of students living off campus by total enrollment. If it's a high ratio — 70% or more is ideal — renter demand in that market is promising. Why is this important? You can keep your rental fully rented, increase rents over time and have the best chance at property appreciation. Beware of extreme ratios, such as less than 10% where everyone lives on campus or virtually 100% where everybody lives at home. Neither extreme makes a good college-town rental market.

Researching various markets is smart for investors. For parents, it's essential. Why? With careful research, investors can avoid the worst markets and buy in the best college towns. Parents, on the other hand, often consider buying a rental only *after* their kid picks a school — and dormitory sticker shock causes panic (not uncommon during the freshman year). *Smart Tip:* Some parents set a college budget limit they will pay based on their state-university rates. Kids can go anywhere they choose, but beyond that budget they will need scholarships, grants and loans. State university towns also tend to be the best rental markets.

Where do you research? Happily, higher education is a highly statistical industry. Besides going directly to the universities ("Housing Office," "Residential Life"), numerous sites aggregate data about institutions, such as *http://www.CollegeData.com*, *http://www.CollegeClickTV.com*, *http://www.CollegeProwler.com*, etc. College Prowler grades housing at 1,000+ schools using student reviews, surveys and public data. Housing is graded on availability, cost, convenience to campus, public transportation and shopping, ease of obtaining, landlords, parking, quality, safety, and variety. *Smart Tip:* That's a useful shopping list for college-town rental buyers, too. Always double-check website figures against a school's latest updates.

Use REIT research. Piggy-back on research by Real Estate Investment Trusts.[††] REITs build large projects, need large demand and favor large public universities in growing states that project increasing college enrollments for the next decade or so. Some of the biggest REITs in this field are American Campus Communities (NYSE: ACC-News), Education Realty Trust (NYSE: EDR-News), and GMH Communities (NYSE: GCT-News). Other large investors include Campus Crest Communities and Prime Properties Investors. Review annual reports online. Look for maps where the REIT has properties and plans future sites, dates built and total beds. Following the big players' moves can be invaluable.

> [††]*Real Estate Investment Trust*
> A publicly traded security that sells like a stock and invests in real estate directly. Equity REITs own or invest in properties and revenue comes principally from rents, while mortgage REITs invest in or make loans and earn money from interest on those loans. Some 90% of REITs are equity REITs that own properties. REITs are a liquid, dividend-paying way to invest in real estate. REITs must distribute 90% of earnings to shareholders by law. *Smart Tip:* If you cringe at tenants who are slobs and engage in endless living-room beer-pong tournaments, investing in publicly traded REITs that specialize in student housing may offer stress-reduced returns.

Use industry data. Since 2010, the National Student Housing Council (NSHC), an affiliate of the National Multi Housing Council (*http://www.NMHC.org*) based in Washington, DC, has collected financial data from its members who play in the $160 billion student housing market. Detailed research is available free to NMHC members and for purchase directly. Want to know what the largest companies (about 30) that own more than 200,000 student housing beds spend on compensation, maintenance, utilities? Here are key takeaways from those national players:

● Many large-property developers have shifted to a per-bed ("individual lease") rather than a per-unit ("standard lease") leasing model.

● In recent years, student properties netted 88.1% of potential rents— only losing 11.9% to vacancies and concessions. Nice numbers.

Use Census figures. One way to make the trend your friend is to focus on states where rising population and secondary school enrollments today mean more college students going to low-cost in-state universities tomorrow. Top growth states include: California, Texas, Florida, New York, Massachusetts, North Carolina, Virginia, Illinois and Georgia.

Use college rankings. Many publications, such as *Bloomberg Business Week, Kiplinger, Smart Money* and *U.S. News & World Report,* publish college rankings. Don't be distracted by "top five-lists" unrelated to housing demand, such as most expensive, highest-paid grads, or even ugliest campus, best music scene or best party schools. Look for college towns high on lists where people are attending schools in large numbers and clamoring to get in. Demand can be revealed by long admission wait lists.

Use housing policy. Avoid markets where schools require on-campus living beyond the first year or two. Private schools are famous for housing almost all their students. They keep the U rooms full by forbidding off-campus living (except perhaps for married or graduate students). At my alma mater, Beloit College in Wisconsin, only 4% of students are permitted to live off-campus. At Princeton only 2% are, and at Vanderbilt (Nashville) only 4% live off-campus. Look for markets where few rooms at the U drive a non-restrictive housing policy, and a large number of students must live in off-campus rentals.

Use university data. Take a prospective student "dorm" tour of campus. Ask admissions for housing costs and the deadlines when housing contracts are due. See if policy requires freshman and/or sophomores or upperclassmen to live on campus. One good sign is a school that requires freshman to live on-campus but typically doesn't have rooms for all of them (first come, first served). Bingo. That means some frosh—and everybody else—will be off-campus renters. Find out if the school offers off-campus housing assistance where landlords can post for-rent properties for free or a fee. (You'll find a whole section on finding tenants in LANDLORD U, Chapter 6.)

CHAPTER 2

Use local media. When students, especially freshmen, can't live on campus, it's news. Subscribe to town and student newspapers and online news sources (for a database of school media: *http://www.CollegeClickTV.com* > college media tab). Check on how many landlords advertise rentals in the student paper/website: little or lots? Keep an eye out for publications/websites and best local rental websites; add to your favorites and set up RSS feeds. Watch for housing fairs to help students find off-campus housing; often these are supported by landlord advertising and exhibits. Get the school's "student housing" updates and set your news filter for keyword-centric sources. Tell-tale signs of a student housing shortage are unhoused students losing in lottery ("dorm draw"), angry parents, dorms cited as obsolete or taken out of service, temporary "purgatory" dorms to house overflow freshmen, renovations breaking the budget or capital plans for athletic or academic facilities rather than housing. Here's why: When old school dorms don't have air conditioning, hi-speed Internet, privacy options, adequate wiring, lighting, ventilation, storage, laundry space — then investors have an opportunity. *Smart Tip:* While tapping school news, watch for old dorms being rehabbed or new dorms being planned that could kill your future flow of tenants.

Use local ordinances. Smart investors know that city, county and local homeowner associations create restrictions to preserve single-family neighborhoods and keep out party houses and college landlords. Keep an eye out for ordinances that ban conversion of existing residences to student housing, restrict occupancy by unrelated persons (max locally varies; often 3 or 4), limits parking places (one unimpeded off-street place per bedroom is a killer) or only grant rental licenses to deed-carrying owners. Before you buy that 5- or 6-bedroom house in a college town, make sure rentals are permitted. Rely on your local real estate agent or trusted mentor. *Smart Tip:* A market that recently defeated a large apartment proposal (500-4,000 bed facility) can be promising for small investors.

Use foreclosure data. Foreclosures are a two-edged sword. On one side, they offer low-cost bargains. On the other, they dampen price appreciation of nearby properties. When first investigating a market, check foreclosure statistics at *http://www.RealtyTrac.com*. Look for two numbers: (1) The average foreclosure discount (difference between the average foreclosure price and the average price of non-foreclosure sales). A 20% to 30% discount is common. The higher the discount, the better the bargains. (2) The percentage of foreclosure sales in the entire market. Here you want enough foreclosures to give you a selection, but not so many that they drag down the whole local market. At its worst during the housing recession, about 30% of all home sales were foreclosures nationwide. A range of 10% to 20% in a college town is a smart opportunity; 4% to 6% is "normal."

SUREFIRE SIGNS OF DEMAND FOR OFF-CAMPUS RENTALS

Although nothing defines demand for your off-campus rentals better than the percentage of students that live off campus, there are other signs:

● **Purgatory dorms:** These are temporary dorms, typically for freshman, at a university that guarantees freshman on-campus living but has more frosh than rooms. Hit by an unexpected wave of acceptances, watch for universities that scramble to create temporary dorms by converting dormitory lounges and multipurpose rooms, or by leasing local hotels, private apartments or complexes, trailer parks or unsold condos.

● **Waiting lists:** Long waiting lists for on-campus housing are another demand indicator that will fill your off-campus rental.

● **Room draw:** Schools that know they have more students than rooms often resort to a lottery system for room assignments. Housing applications are submitted in an open period, often online, then rooms are assigned either by selection (complex ranking criteria) or lottery. Disappointed students rent off-campus. Lots of them.

● **Aged campus & off-campus housing:** There's a lot to be said for campus life: simplicity, convenience, social scene, community, randomly seeing friends at meals, lower cost, no need for car expenses or parking hassles. Yet, given a choice, most students prefer to live off-campus for privacy, independence, more space and higher GPA. To those students, quality, age and type of school housing is a big deal. For many big schools, the last big dorm-building era was the 1970s and 1980s, to house the Baby Boomers. That also means much of the close-in off-campus housing was built long ago. Not only do older properties need more maintenance and possibly rehab, but modern upgrades are needed, too. *Smart Tip:* Look for schools with vintage dorms, maybe even obsolete or some being taken out of service and no capital funds planned for renovation or expansion. Ancient dorms drive up rental demand and are a close second behind no rooms at the U for investors.

● **Developable sites:** One way to minimize competition in a market from deep-pocket developers is finding locations where land sites are not available or not large enough. Lack of developable parcels can keep the big players from siphoning off your student renters, stifling rents and appreciation. That can be an outstanding plus in favor of a college-town market. *Smart Tip:* Be shy about investing in a college town with lots of new construction. Building is a flag that the market has been "discovered" and a "developer's welcome" sign has been hung out by the university and local authorities. Many land-grant colleges have lots of room for expansion, and developers build complexes with free shuttle service to campus.

● **Small town:** For out-of-town investors planning to specialize in a college town, you must realize that the local real estate fraternity is small. Expect everyone to know each other: real estate agents, lenders, investor owners, attorneys, inspectors, title reps, town clerks, property managers, etc. Some will have gone to grade school together. You're the outsider. Cultivate a reputation of being reasonable, fair and informed. Don't set out to show the locals how it's done right where you come from. There are no secrets. What goes around comes around in small-town college real estate. *Smart Tip:* Consider using your first (small) deal to leave the impression that you are a fair player. After all, you want to be among the first to be called when the next great deal pops up.

10 ESSENTIAL SIGNS OF A GREAT COLLEGE-TOWN REAL ESTATE MARKET

Look first at the school, then the town, to find the right college market for your investment:

1. More than 70% of students live off campus.

2. Living off-campus is unrestricted by school housing policy.

3. Large public university ($\sim$7,500–15,000 students) with majority full-time (12–18 credit hours per semester) and high out-of-state and international-student ratio.

4. College enrollment projected to increase steadily, not capped by policy.

5. University-owned housing is vintage, out-of-date, most built in the 20th century or earlier.

6. State population projected to grow steadily.

7. Little to no new-construction apartment complexes being built or planned.

8. Absence of multiple major national players developing "purpose built" apartments (i.e., big players control less than 10% of off-campus beds).

9. No signs of overbuilt market, declining rents or reduced demand.

10. College town has lots of related businesses, research facilities, hospitals, international presence that creates parellel non-student rental demand.

Costly Mistakes To Avoid Buying In The Wrong College Market

Mistake #1: Commuter Campuses. At first glance, some large schools have amazingly high (like 100%) off-campus housing numbers. Don't get tripped up by commuter schools and for-profit telecommuter universities with virtually no campus housing. You can spot these campuses from their website because the Student Housing section is missing or minimal. For example, the largest university in America is the Northern Virginia Community College (NOVA) system (more than 67,000 students with almost 100% living off-campus in the Washington, DC market). The four campuses have no dorms because students don't live on or near campus. They live at home. Near NOVA's campuses close-in, student housing is almost non-existent . . . as are the investment opportunities. See for yourself on Google Maps. Where a residential campus has dormitory housing, a commuter campus has parking lots.

Make no mistake: Full-time versus part-time is another flag for investors because FT students drive rental demand, where PT students typically live at home or commute beyond the two-mile radius of "student housing." Also PT students tend to be employed full-time (35 hours a week) and go to school part-time. Their life focus is off

CHAPTER 2

COLLEGE TOWNS 101

campus, not on student life. Without demand, it will be harder to rent your investment, tough to raise rents and appreciation will be lower. *Smart Tip:* Watch for a commuter college that is actively transforming into a traditional four-year university. Growth in housing demand will be steady for years to come.

Mistake #2: Not recognizing a decline in enrollment. Success for the college-town buy-to-rent strategy is rising enrollment. States that are losing population, in the future will have fewer scholars to send to universities. Declining enrollment reduces rental demand. When a school's academic standing is downgraded, or a scandal, tragedy, or bad publicity strikes a particular university — from sports recruiting to shooting rampages to child molesting — enrollment can suffer. Another variation of this demand killer is when an institution caps enrollment for budget or capacity. Whatever the reason, flat or declining enrollment reduces market demand for rentals. *Smart Tip:* You can spot a downward trend early in sinking applications, admissions and transfer numbers.

Mistake #3: Trying to compete against REITs and new construction. This is no small matter. Today there are so many developers and real estate investment trusts that specialize in student housing ("publicly traded multi-family REITs") that demand has spawned several trade associations, conferences, and industry publications to serve the niche. Some resource-strapped universities see opportunity in exchanging premier location on or near campus for long-term contracts with developers to build and manage "purpose built" student apartment complexes. These developers are smart. They listen to their customers (students and university) and deliver a hotel experience (also, "country club," "resort") chockfull of amenities in large apartment communities, often 250–750 beds — all designed to beat other landlords to guaranteed tenants. Their economies of scale — and sometimes special incentives from community zoning or tax breaks or university approved housing status (think — university rules guaranteeing their beds are full, not yours) — that make it difficult for the small investor to compete. While you can get smart watching what college towns the REITs target, be cautious about buying in their shadow. *Smart Tip:* New construction will always make older properties look — well — older. By not overpaying in the first place, and by paying down or eliminating your mortgage loan, you'll be able to price competitively against the new guy who has to pay today's higher land, construction and other acquisition costs.

Mistake #4: Ignoring a market's danger signs that can kill rental demand.

Danger signs:

▶ High vacancies.

▶ Declining rents — local landlords lowering rents to compete with new mega-properties that offer 10-month leases (rather than 12-month) and incentives (discounts) such as utilities bundled in the rent and free hi-speed Wi-Fi.

▶ Numerous rental properties come on the market in a short time (read: panic sell off).

▶ Many investment-property foreclosures (worse still are many foreclosures of newly constructed private homes).

Common causes:

▶ Overbuilt market or large apartment community planned or being built next to campus.

▶ Enrollment declines due to tougher entrance requirements (test scores, grade-point averages), higher fees or reduced reputation from scandal.

▶ Sudden reversal in university policy not allowing students to live off campus.

▶ University announces policy to move toward online distance learning (popular, convenient and often more profitable for universities), rather than on-campus attendance.

▶ New university opens in state or nearby.

Smart Tip: None of these trends are good for the college landlord. Your best solution is not to buy in that market in the first place. When it comes time to sell your rental years from now, the lack of buyers (they recognize the drop in demand) could kill any hopes of an appreciable profit.

Mistake #5: Buying because you're a football fan or alumnus.

Your heart may be in the right place, but college housing is business. Do your due diligence to make sure the property and the numbers add up to a sound investment. Remember: A shortage of on-campus dorms and a growing enrollment are essential to reaching 100% occupancy and price appreciation when it comes time to cash out down the road. If your property is near state-of-the-art healthcare and entertainment facilities (but not necessarily on top of them), that's a plus to more buyers than just other football fans or college parent-investors.

Mistake #6: Not watching the student loan trends like a hawk.
Student loan debt has reached nearly $1 trillion. Some doomsayers
warn that student loan defaults could be the next credit bubble to burst
(and others fret that debt will keep first-time home buyers from buying
at all). Down on earth, a smart investor keeps an eye on the student-loan
interest rates. Given that the average four-year degree student graduates
with about $25,000 in student debt, a dramatic increase in interest rates
could make college even more expensive. So far, government subsidies
keep student rates relatively low (private loans are typically at market
rates). *Smart Tip:* If subsidies end or rates rise beyond affordable limits,
take it as a trigger to sell before your cash cow curdles. Student housing
may be relatively recession resistant, but not even college towns are
change-proof.

Another trend to watch for college-town rentals is the retirement
crowd. If you don't want to retire there, maybe there's a boomer
generation itching to buy your property when the time is right.
Where? Think Gainesville FL, Fort Collins CO, Columbia MO,
Asheville NC, Chapel Hill NC, Logan UT, Charlottesville VA and
Missoula, MT. But first we need to find a goldmine property . . . and
that's just what you'll learn in the next chapter.

Chapter 2 Roundup

**Smart Essentials COLLEGE TOWNS 101 ::
What You Have Learned**

▶▶ How to spot a good college-town market.

▶▶ Surefire signs of demand for off-campus rentals.

▶▶ 10 essential signs of a great college-town real
estate market.

▶▶ Costly mistakes to avoid buying in the wrong
college market.

CHAPTER 3
GOLDMINES

In this chapter, you'll learn smart ways to:

1. **Recognize locations that produce profitable student rentals today.**

2. **Find college-town properties that are worth buying.**

3. **Avoid all-too-common property picking mistakes that cost serious money.**

After selecting your market, the essential principle of real estate is location, location, location. Besides prices, safe neighborhood, and rising enrollment trends, the first essential factor to look for is being nearby the school.

LOCATION: WHERE TO LOOK FOR PROFITABLE STUDENT RENTALS

Think waterfront. The university is an ocean of students. The coastline is the campus boundary. If the property has a "view of the U," it is the most desirable, and that's reflected in a higher property value and a higher rental premium, just like beachfront property. Property values close-in may command a 15%-20% premium over driving-distance properties. Move away from the "waterfront," and the next Circle of Value is "walkable," which generally means within a mile or a 30-minute walking distance (think of 18 to 20-somethings sprinting from bed to an 8 a.m. class in under 7 minutes). Watch for rentals being described as "X-minute walk to campus."

Next is the "bikeable" ring, perhaps within one to three miles — or about a 10-minute bike ride — or along bus or light-rail routes. It's not uncommon for walkable and bikeable properties to sell for a 5% – 7% price bump. Beyond those premium locations is the rest of the universe of drivable locations within 10 – 15 miles to campus parking. Forget waterfront premiums: These properties sell for regular comparable prices. *Smart Tip:* Properties within the walk/bike zone don't need as many parking spaces, if any at all. Rentals farther out require parking — sometimes requiring one-space-per-bedroom rather than one-space-per-unit. Traffic from high student density is one reason communities often have permit and parking rules that restrict student housing. Make sure student renters are allowed to get neighborhood parking permits if you're considering a property outside the walk/bike zone.

● **Study the campus map.** Note where the classroom buildings are located, where the athletic facilities sit, where large off-campus student parking lots cluster (shuttles to campus?) and where the university built its student housing. Now look at nearby neighborhoods. What you will see — particularly with behemoth campuses the size of a small town — is that some locations are better than others for campus access. The residential "shore" often has a strip of bars, pizza joints, hair salons/spas, take-outs and coffee shops. You'll also notice that access to particular schools — med school with hospital or the law, engineering or business schools — define premium locations. Rental properties nearby those facilities will tend to appeal to that type of student. Would you rather rent to a med student who studies 24/7 or an undergraduate who parties 24/7? You get the idea. Location, location, location. If you must buy miles from campus, make sure there is transportation (students without cars are often the biggest users of college-town bus systems). Study the area bus route map and find out whether the university offers a bus or shuttle service.

● **Think multiple locations.** If one property is far from campus and one is closer, the close-to-school property is better (assuming neighborhoods and numbers are equal). Be sure the property is located where demand for rentals is high from your target pool: students or staff, faculty, professionals. *Smart Tip:* Think twice before putting "all your eggs in one basket" if you want to buy more than one college-town property. Buying in different neighborhoods can diversify your portfolio. Having investments in different locations around a college town allows you to benefit if one area appreciates rapidly while another location becomes a bust.

◆ ◆ ◆

Essential Takeaway: *A location close to the center of campus is ideal. Close-in and walkable properties will appreciate the best, rent faster and command higher rents. Being close to campus is so essential that the location can even trump other shortcomings in a property, such as scarce parking or vintage construction.*

> *Yet, always buy the smart cash-flow deal even if it doesn't overlook the campus "waterfront," as you'll learn ever-so shortly in COLLEGE MATH (Chapter 4).*

◆ ◆ ◆

PROPERTY: FINDING PROPERTY THAT MAKES YOU MONEY

You never know when a great college-town rental deal will hit the market. Be patient. Be ready. Whack that mole when opportunity pops up. Remember: It's not uncommon for smart investors to look at a dozen deals — or more — before buying one.

A high ratio of students living off campus — 70% or higher — is paramount for renter demand. Affordable property values are also essential. That's why large public universities in small college towns are often the best investment opportunity. But the devil is in the details. Bad investment properties are everywhere. Finding the good ones is the secret. Put another way: It's smarter to get a good deal with cash-flow in a not-so-great location than overpaying for a great location in a great market for a property that's a money-losing investment. Simply: Price, cash flow and return are essential.

10 Smart Ways To Find Property Worth Buying

1. Find a top local agent and property manager. Drive around. Note for-sale and property-management signs on buildings. Note ads in the student newspaper. or online classifieds (think Craigslist, etc.).

In college towns, investment student housing is often dominated by two to three brokerage and management firms. *Smart Tip:* Show your agent that you're serious. Get on a broker's email property-alert system with your criteria and you will be notified when new rental properties for sale come on the market.

2. Meet with property management companies, especially those affiliated with a real estate brokerage, and ask them to contact you when clients want to sell. Be specific about the type of property you want.

3. Study who owns the best student housing in town. Expect local investors to own most of the properties. Meet the principals. Owners

of good properties won't want to sell a good thing. Be patient. Life events such as estate planning, bad partners, maxed-out depreciation or sudden need for cash can turn owners into sellers. You want to be the first person they call.

4. Expect locals to ask if you own any properties near the campus. If you have made your first buy, you're no longer a tire kicker, especially if you use your own money. Locals will then take you seriously, even if it's a smaller property. Next, spread the word that you want to expand your holdings. One good place to do this is by joining the local landlords or apartment-owners association.

5. Specialize in one aspect of one market, whether single-family houses, townhouses, condominiums, "plexes" (duplexes, triplexes, quads), or small apartment buildings (1–10 units) with separate electric meters. (Once you own two or more student rentals you can spread costs and vacancies over more units.) Your offspring and their friends might even occupy one of the units. Keep in mind that single-family houses traditionally have the greatest resale market — another investor, the current renter, or a live-in owner.

6. Become a student of sales prices of similar properties using universal denominators to build your sense of market value, such as the appraiser shorthand that compares total rooms, total bedrooms, total baths (i.e., "7-3-2") or classified ad lingo for multi-family (i.e., "four 1/1's" = one building with four 1-bedroom, 1-bath apartments).

7. Look for a close-to-campus neighborhood with a low crime rate and where nearby properties are well-maintained. Concentrate your search in the median-to-lower price ranges that can be supported with rents. Look for broad rental appeal, which will also appeal to the widest range of prospective buyers when you're ready to sell.

8. Search for student housing that doesn't require a lot of maintenance or can be cosmetically improved with not much more than paint and carpet, and has solid construction and sturdy appliances.

9. Watch for sellers less interested in getting the max price than they are in just getting out of the property quickly: (1) Investors who have depreciated a rental to the max; (2) investors who face emergency cash need; or (3) distressed owners facing foreclosure, who may be more motivated by a fast sale than the bottom line.

10. Compare rents for similar student units nearby. One handy rule-of-thumb is rental rate per bedroom (rent divided by bedrooms = rent per bedroom). Newbie investors are often surprised at the relatively small range between low and high rental rates for similar-size units in a community.

◆ ◆ ◆

Essential Takeaway: *Of course, there is no perfect world. Know your "walkaway price" and be prepared to walk away if a property is overpriced. That said: Reconsider if the property is within a block or two of campus. Location, location, location commands higher rents and easier leasing.*

◆ ◆ ◆

What To Look For In Perfect College Rental Properties

💬 **Fixer-Uppers:** Finding close-in low-price single-family rental homes for sale near a big university takes work. One essential step is to determine how much it will cost to keep/make them rentable. Rehab costs can easily be more than the selling price. One proven strategy to create instant equity is to increase a property's capacity, such as convert a basement, porch, attic or garage into an extra bedroom or two, or build an addition. Keep in mind that those capital costs can sink your investment in red ink—unless renovation delivers greater rental income (higher rent, more beds) and increased property value. Be sure addition/renovation plans comply with local ordinances before undertaking renovations—or buying the property.

Smart Tip: When maintenance has been put off, professional, independent inspections are essential. Be sure your inspectors are not more beholden to their referral source, such as the listing agent or local lender, than to you, their occasional client. Next you'll need to translate any shortcomings into a firm quote for contractor work, not a WAG (wild-ass guess). Improvements range from code (make it habitable) to cosmetic (carpet, paint, kitchen, baths) to down-to-the-studs rehab (electrical, mechanical, roof, new layout). *Smart Tip:* If a prospective property doesn't have Wi-Fi or wired HSIA ("ethernet"), consider installing it. Caveat: If the school Wi-Fi hot zone reaches the location already and is powerful enough to support heavy use indoors 24/7, then you may dodge the Wi-Fi bullet.

● **Kiddie Condos:** The significantly higher cost of single family homes coupled with the regular maintenance that a house requires (especially close-in vintage properties built in the last century when the university was younger), leads many investors and parents to consider a less-expensive and more "worry-free" student condo. Condos are developed for owners; apartments are developed for renters. That's one reason college condos are appealing, especially to first-time investors, parents and enterprising students. Management is provided, and running the numbers on price and costs is relatively straight forward. Tracking condo resale values is easier when you buy because there often are several other closely comparable units to compare. Most college condos are two or three bedrooms or whatever falls within local laws against renting to unrelated tenants. Look for condos with three or four bedrooms or with large bedrooms that fit two students per bedroom. If the condo only allots one parking space per unit, try to make nearby rent-a-space arrangements with other owners.

No way around it: Low interest rates and condo prices that are lower than single-family houses can add up to monthly payments that are lower than monthly rents, even after including the condo fee. One or two extra bedrooms to rent out at a close-in, amenity-loaded facility may pay most expenses — but not all — to offset your offspring's "free rent." Condo fees cover exterior and common-area maintenance, and property insurance (very nice for out-of-area parents). Owner maintenance is reduced to what's inside the unit. Newer condos tend to require less expense as property maintenance mostly involves room-turnover upkeep. If you can sweeten your numbers with mortgage interest deductions and other tax breaks — plus the promise of equity buildup from loan pay-down or long-term appreciation after resale costs — owning a condo can start looking better than renting a place for your scholar or committing to a dorm.

Smart Tip: Treat your child's college years as one lump sum. Say you would pay dorm/rent payments for three years (36 months) to graduation at $550/month, or a total of $19,800 out-of-pocket. You may instead be able to buy a condo where extra rents and tax deductions break even with expenses, and (optimistically) 8% appreciation over three years washes out resale costs. Voila! Zero out of pocket. You just saved $19,800. Was the risk worth it? (1) Run your own numbers.

(2) Make sure your scholar will stick it out four years at the same U.
(3) You'll know in hindsight.

Caution: There are pros and cons of condo investing. Although condos can be attractive — especially for price-to-rent ratios — to a greater extent than other property types, your investment return at condo resale will be greatly affected by the actions of others beyond your control. The attractiveness and value of your property could be impacted by these (and other) heartburns:

▶ Good or bad condo management.

▶ Poor selection of tenants by other condo owners.

▶ Sell-offs by other owners.

▶ Multiple competing units for sale that are similar, if not identical.

▶ High percentage of unsold or unrented units.

▶ Multiple or long-term vacancies or foreclosures throughout the complex.

▶ Developer bankruptcy.

Smart Tip: Watch out for a high proportion of occupant owners. Buyers that intend to live there often pay prices that are as much as they can afford. But as an investor, you must focus on cash flow, loan payments, expenses, and return on investment. Paying too much for a property is the worst mistake novice investors make. If the numbers don't show cash flow, keep looking for a condo deal that will make you money.

● **Walk-Bike-Bus-Drive:** Although more a location factor than a property factor, public transportation virtually at a property's doorstep can be important. Fannie Mae considers this essential. To qualify for Fannie Mae's Dedicated Student Housing Loan Program, properties must be located within two miles of the campus or on a university-sanctioned bus line. As we said earlier, properties within walking/biking distance or on a bus line (preferably direct) generate higher revenue because close-in tenants can ditch car-related costs — and some of those costs can be used to pay rent. If a property is beyond the two-mile walk-bike limit, be sure it's on a bus line.

All Things Equal: Which Is The Smarter Property To Buy?

Picture two college properties: Both require the same cash investment, both generate the same cash flow, both have the identical future sale price. Which one is the better investment? Or put another way: What risks will affect the ultimate return? Although smart analysis is as much art as science, the more you can quantify your risks, the more winners you'll land from the lake full of losers.

● **Occupancy matters.** Occupancy is the flip side of vacancy. If the property is currently a rental, get a five-year rental history (ask for leases and income statements). Proven high occupancy can trump a closer-in location (100% is ideal; 1 month empty per year = 92% occupancy; 2 months lost = 83% occupancy; 3 months = 75% occupancy). Check out occupancy rates in the area. Ask how long properties stay on the rental market. In some areas, condos, townhouses or multi-family units may be easier to rent than single-family homes. In other areas, the reverse may be true. Buy the property that rents fastest and stays occupied.

● **Age matters.** Older properties cost more to maintain. Over the years, higher expenses result in lower cash flows. It's better to buy the newer property or the one that's in good shape and easy to maintain. Avoid properties that need expensive repairs or replacements just to be rentable, which can seriously impact the profitability of your investment. Since investment homes are often sold "as is" — meaning you, the new owner, will be responsible for bringing the property up to standards for rentals in the area — you can minimize your financial outlay by selecting a property that does not require extensive structural repairs or major improvements.

● **Resale matters.** Investing in a better neighborhood can offer more potential for a faster sale or lease-purchase than an investment located in a less desirable neighborhood. Obviously, preference goes to the property with the best resale potential. Research a property's past (*http://www.Zillow.com* > property history). Look to the future. Find out from your agent, mentor and other investors/landlords what plans are underway to change the living-off-campus housing percentage and the neighborhood (e.g., road construction, new homes) that might affect the value or demand for your investment. *Smart Tip:* High home-turnover areas may indicate rental neighborhoods, which typically appreciate slower than owner-occupied homes . . . and sometimes depreciate. For resale, choose a property in a more-stable neighborhood among owner-occupied homes.

● **Amenities matter.** Every rental has competition. When shopping, keep in mind how to make your rental better than the next. Can you afford to offer an all-inclusive rent, like some apartments often do, with a bundled utility package including electricity, gas/oil, water, sewer, cable, high-speed Wi-Fi? Is there a washer/dryer in the unit? Reserved or covered parking? If not, can you budget to improve or add amenities and take the property up a notch?

◆ ◆ ◆

Essential Takeaway: *There's no single magic formula to college properties. Every deal is different. The right research and right financing are essential. We're believers in patient money: buy and hold for income. We also think owning multiple properties is better than owning one (see Mistake #3 below). A little more than 40% of investors purchase more than one property, National Association of REALTORS® research shows. There's a smart reason for that.*

◆ ◆ ◆

Costly Property Picking Mistakes To Avoid

Mistake #1: Not planning for the unexpected expense.

Solution: Even with your best projections and using previous years' figures, the only thing that nails operating expenses is experience — and even experience can get blown out of the water by the unforeseen. Here are the key factors to watch like a hawk. Vacancy rates: Is there some market-level trend, such as lower enrollments, making renting harder? Energy costs: Are heating or air conditioning or water/sewer costs skyrocketing? Insurance: Is your market in a zone for hurricanes, tornados, floods, earthquakes, mud slides? Real estate taxes: Is the local tax jurisdiction aiming to balance its ravaged budget on the backs of property owners? *Smart Tip:* If several major cost factors have converged on a candidate property, consider another property (or market) for your equity, sweat and time.

Mistake #2: Not tending to safety issues.

Solution: Yes, some students drink a lot and party like crazy. What else? They get into trouble. If the trouble is tenants or their guests breaking any law, call the police. If it's partying, be sure your property is safe.

Provide secure doors, locks, peepholes, alarms for smoke and carbon monoxide and fire extinguishers and decks or balconies with reinforced railings strong enough to support more college kids per square foot than can fit into a party bus. Be sure the electric service is juiced for amp overload.

Mistake #3: Buying one expensive property instead of two less-expensive ones.

Solution: Imagine the dilemma of spending your cash to buy one higher-priced property or two less-costly ones. Smart investors know you're better off with two lower priced properties, for example, buying two $100,000 townhomes rather than one $200,000 single-family house. Why? A twice-the-price property typically doesn't pull twice the rent, but it may cost twice as much in mortgage payments, taxes, upkeep, etc. Also, unexpected big expenses and contingency reserves (vacancies, improvements) aren't as gut-kicking when spread over more than one property. *Smart Tip:* If you have the cash to make two down payments, and two sets of closing costs and rehab expenses, then the smart investor strategy is to buy two properties not one.

Enough big picture, let's get down to the bottom line you'll need to know before sending your real estate money to college. You'll learn plenty about how to analyze a good buy once you run the numbers in the next chapter, COLLEGE MATH.

Chapter 3 Roundup

Smart Essentials GOLDMINES ::
What You Have Learned

▶▶ Smart locations to look for profitable student rentals.
▶▶ How to find property that makes you money.
▶▶ 10 smart ways to spot property worth buying.
▶▶ What to look for in perfect student rental properties.
▶▶ All things equal: Which is the smarter property to buy?
▶▶ Costly property picking mistakes to avoid.

CHAPTER 4
COLLEGE MATH

In this chapter, you'll learn smart ways to:

1. Target a strategy that works for you — and stick to it.

2. Separate profitable rentals from money pits with surefire analysis techniques.

3. Negotiate contract contingencies to craft win-win purchase offers.

ANALYZING A GOLDMINE WHEN YOU FIND ONE

Return on your college-rental investment is calculated two ways: (1) cash flow and (2) long-term appreciation. Ideally you want to make money both ways. Run the numbers to get an answer to these two questions: (1) How much income can you expect? and (2) What rate of return on your cash investment will the property yield?

For cash flow, smart parents and investors first look at "price-to-rent" ratios, then run the numbers for cash flow "before taxes" and "after taxes." For rate of return, one evaluation is "cash on cash" that primarily compares price with a number of other key factors. Another more-technical analysis is the "internal rate of return" that compares ultimate return against the cash you invested.

Keep in mind: All your numbers will be based on educated guesses. Every analysis is only as good as its assumptions. In the real-world, only experience with a property will give you truly accurate figures. For now, depend on your top agent, mentor and financial/tax advisors for data, and when in doubt, lean toward conservative numbers.

> **5 Key Assumptions That Impact Your Numbers**

◗ Purchase costs. You'll need to consider how much money you have to invest in down payment, closing costs ("cash invested," "equity cash investment"), and rehab costs to make a property rentable. Total all three costs together to know your "all in" cash-invested figure.

CHAPTER 4

COLLEGE MATH

● **Ownership costs.** As you budget, allow for operating expenses, such as principal, interest, escrows[††] for insurance and real estate taxes, maintenance and other operating expenses (one rule of thumb pegs all costs at 33% of rental income). Then add property management fees (if any, typically 3%-10% of rents), plus utilities (if not paid by tenant), and income taxes. Make sure to set aside a reserve fund in your guesstimate to cover unexpected repairs (one monthly rent or 10% of annual rents is common), and expect at least 1 to 3 months of vacancy between rentals.

> **[††] *Escrows***
>
> Escrows are funds paid each month by a borrower to a lender or loan servicer to cover the lump sum payments due throughout the year for taxes and hazard insurance. The lender/loan servicer holds these funds in a non-interest-bearing account. Expect this figure to fluctuate over the years.

● **Financing costs.** How you finance the purchase (if not paying all-cash) will significantly affect your monthly payment figure. The size of your down payment is based on what you can afford. If the property has been a rental long enough, your mortgage lender may allow you to factor a portion of the property's average rental cash flow into your income to boost your borrowing power.

● **Income.** You'll need to set a competitive rental price ("fair market rent") and calculate your income with an assumption that you will have occasional vacancies between renters. With due diligence, you'll nail down the Net Operating Income (NOI) estimate, including rent, and possible ancillary income from late fees, laundry, parking, vending machines, utility reimbursements or forfeited damage deposits. You'll also subtract for vacancies, uncollectable rents. Next subtract operating expenses, including mortgage, taxes, insurance, utilities, repairs, maintenance including turn-over costs, plus outside services such as lawn care, snow removal, cleaning, supplies, advertising, and admin expenses. Lastly, take away fees for professional services for legal, accounting, property management, etc. Be sure to include improvements ("capital expenditures"), contingency reserves and reasonable return on cash invested. That leaves you with an estimated income statement. To give you starter figures: Industry vacancy forecasts range from 7.5% (best case), 10% (expected), 12.5% (worst case). But remember, one

CHAPTER 4

COLLEGE MATH

month vacancy = 8.3% lost income, two months = 16.7%, three months = 25% of income lost. If your kid lives there, be sure to calculate that "free rent" into your vacancy factor.

● **Taxes.** Don't forget to factor tax breaks into your budget. Most property owners can take a tax deduction for mortgage interest, property taxes and a variety of other expenses, as well as depreciate the value of the home every year. For authoritative information on tax issues, consult your tax advisor and see IRS Publication 527, "Residential Rental Property."

◆ ◆ ◆

Essential Takeaway: *Numerous excellent software programs are available to help with investment-property analysis. Get one. Ask your real estate agent, your accountant, property manager, mentor or other landlords. Remember: You may not be able to cover all the costs in the first few years of ownership. That doesn't necessarily mean it's a bad investment. By holding the property long enough, inflation may increase the rents you can charge, eventually generating enough income to exceed expenses. In addition, the best properties increase in value over time, rewarding owners with capital gains upon sale, especially if the acquisition price is a below-market bargain. Patient money wins the race.*

◆ ◆ ◆

Four Essential Numbers To Run A Smart Property Analysis

Here are the essential principles at play in analyzing any investment property.

Number #1: Price-To-Rent
Smart investors compare properties by looking at their "price-to-rent" ratios (P/R) as a first rule-of-thumb (also, "gross rent multiplier" or GRM). Simply divide the listing price of the property by the annual rent you can expect to receive from it.

Example: $100,000 price by $10,800 annual rent = 9.3 P/R ratio. Compare that to a similar-size property priced at $75,000 for the same $10,800 rent = 6.9 P/R ratio. The lower the number, the better the investment deal—assuming all other factors are equal.

You can also use the P/R ratio to flag the best areas to invest in and to compare one college-town market with another. Moody's (*http://www.Economy.com*) regularly ranks 54 metro areas nationally by P/R ratio, and *http://www.Zillow.com* offers "rent Zestimates®" for specific properties. But current, local figures are essential to sharpen your numbers.

◆ ◆ ◆

Essential Takeaway: *The best college rentals often fall in the 10 to 15 price-to-rent range, which reflects relatively high rents and low property values. Hot or not, the P/R ratio is a ballpark tool at best. Real bean counters use the capitalization rate ("cap rate") as a more accurate valuation tool. Rather than gross rent, cap rate uses net operating income (NOI) after subtracting expenses and vacancy factors. Whatever formula you use, be careful to compare values for similar property types, and especially avoid comparing sales prices of rental homes to owner-occupied homes—that's apples to oranges with different underlying values. Using closed sale prices, rather than listing prices, also increases accuracy.*

◆ ◆ ◆

Number #2: Cash-on-Cash Return

A cash-on-cash (CoC) return (also, "return on investment" or ROI) is the property's annual net cash flow divided by your net investment. CoC is a rough but useful back-of-the-envelope exercise. It tells you how much cash your investment is putting in your pocket.

💬 25% Down Cash-on-Cash Example

Assume the following: You buy a $100,000 investment property, put down 25% or $25,000, your mortgage is $75,000, and you have a principal and interest payment of $375 monthly. In addition, you invest another 5% or $5,000 for closing costs, loan pre-paids and fix-up repairs. Your all-in cash invested ("buyer's equity") starts at $30,000 ($25,000 + $5,000 = $30,000).

▶ Rent Monthly: $900

▶ Expenses Monthly: –$300 [33.3% of rent]

▶ Net Operating Income: $600

▶ Monthly Loan Payment: –$375

▶ Monthly Net Income: $225

▶ Annual Net Income: $2,700

▶ Cash Invested: $30,000

▶ Cash-on-Cash Return: 9% first year [$2,700 divided by $30,000]

● 100% Down Cash-on-Cash Example

Assume you buy the same $100,000 property but put down 100% ("all cash") and add $3,000 in fix-ups ($100,000 + $3,000 fix-ups = $103,000); you'll have no loan or pre-paids. The scenario gives you significantly greater monthly cash flow.

▶ Rent Monthly: $900

▶ Expenses Monthly: –$300 [33.3% of rent]

▶ Net Operating Income: $600

▶ Monthly Loan Payment: –$0

▶ Monthly Net Income: $600

▶ Annual Net Income: $7,200

▶ Cash Invested: $103,000

▶ Cash-on-Cash Return: 7% first year [$7,200 divided by $103,000]

See the tradeoff? Annual income is much greater in this all-cash example ($7,200 versus $2,700), yet the 25%-down example delivers a better first-year CoC return percentage (9% vs. 7%). All cash, of course, assumes you have the money to buy the property outright. In addition, your cash risk is bigger in the all-cash example because your leverage ("other people's money") is smaller, in fact, zero.

◆ ◆ ◆

Essential Takeaway: *As you analyze more properties, a sharp pencil will reveal what other investors have learned: Sought-after properties, like high-end or waterfront or fancy condos, generally have lower—or negative—cash-on-cash returns compared to moderate- to low-priced properties that offer higher positive cash flows.* Smart Tip: *Go for the cash flow, not the prize properties.*

◆ ◆ ◆

Number #3: Internal Rate of Return (IRR)

Internal rate of return (also, "annual percentage yield") is the total true return on your investment taking into account depreciation, appreciation and equity gained from paying down the debt.

Essential assumptions for 25%-down example:

- ▶ Net Income: $225 monthly [$2,700 per year]
- ▶ Property Value: $100,000
- ▶ Initial Cash Investment: $30,000 [$25,000 down + $5,000 pre-paids and fix-ups]
- ▶ Depreciation (first year): $2,900 [MACRS-GDS[††]: $80,000 base divided by 27.5. Assume the property is put into service in January, thus qualifying for 12-month depreciation in the first year. Because the remaining depreciable property value declines every year, accelerated depreciation also declines every year.]
- ▶ Marginal Tax Bracket: 28% [28% and above makes real estate tax breaks most attractive]
- ▶ Appreciation: 6% that first year [$6,000]
- ▶ Principal Pay-Down: $1,200 first year

[††]*MACRS-GDS*
The letters stand for Modified Accelerated Cost Recovery System-General Depreciation System, the current US tax depreciation system. See IRS Publication 946, "How To Depreciate Property."

Internal Rate of Return Example:

► Net Income: $2,700
► Depreciation Value: $812 [Tax Savings: $2,900 depreciation x 28% tax bracket]
► Appreciation: $6,000 [$100,000 x 6%]
► Principal Pay-Down: $1,200 [$100 x 12 months]
► Total Internal Rate of Return: $10,712 [sum of the above amounts]
► Internal Rate of Return (first year): 36% [$10,712 divided by $30,000 initial investment]

Keep in mind: Unlike cash-on-cash analysis, total internal rate of return is not spendable cash. Figuring a true return is tricky. *Smart Tip:* If you have positive cash-on-cash return before taxes, your IRR percentage will always be an even better number.

◆ ◆ ◆

Essential Takeaway: *All forecasts are built on key assumptions: financing, rehab costs, rents, vacancies, depreciation rules and marginal tax rates, maintenance costs, management fees. If one assumption—or several—proves wrong, the tables easily turn. Expect high rents? Low vacancies? High tax breaks? Low expenses? Smart investors treat forecasts as a navigation chart to a destination. Along the way they regularly make mid-course corrections to miss the icebergs that drift into their path.*

◆ ◆ ◆

Number #4: Cash Flow Before And After Taxes

The most universal reckoning of success in investment properties, especially for hold-for-income landlords, is analysis of a property's cash flow before and after taxes. This greatly simplified example makes clear the impact of depreciation and other tax breaks on your cash-flow numbers.

COLLEGE MATH

Essential Assumptions:

- ▶ Cost of Property: $100,000
- ▶ Cash Invested: $30,000 [$25,000 down + $5,000 closing and fix-up costs]
- ▶ Financing: $75,000 for 30 years; monthly payment for principal and interest $375
- ▶ Monthly Rent: $900
- ▶ Annual Rent: $10,800
- ▶ Depreciable Base: $80,000 [Improvements (buildings, landscaping, etc.) assumed to be 80% of sale price]
- ▶ Depreciation (1st year): $2,900
- ▶ Marginal Tax Rate: 28%

Cash Flow Before Taxes
All figures are annual for first year.

1. Annual Income: $7,200 [$10,800 rent – $3,600 expenses]

2. Principal: $1,300 [Paid principal ("amortization") is not a taxable expense because payments increase your equity. Because it is a cash outlay, principal is an operating expense.]

3. Interest Expense: $3,000

4. Taxes: $1,500

5. Insurance: $500 [Including hazard, liability, private mortgage insurance, credit life, credit disability, etc.]

6. Operating Expenses: $1,080 [10% annual rent includes: accounting, leasing, and legal fees, property management, maintenance, repairs, services, supplies, miscellaneous]

7. Improvements: $1,080 [10% annual rent]

8. Reserve: $1,080 [10% annual rent for vacancy/non-payment losses and emergency repairs]

9. Annual Expenses Sub-Total: $9,540 [Add #2 through #8]

10. **Cash Flow Before Tax: – $2,340** [$7,200 (#1) – $9,540 (#9) = – $2,340 (loss)]

Return Before Tax: – 7.8% [– $2,340 cash flow before tax (#10) divided by $30,000 cash invested.]

Cash Flow After Taxes
Again, all figures are annual for first year.

11. Cash Flow Before Tax: –$2,340

12. Principal: $1,300 [Remove principal, a cash outlay that is not taxable, from cash flow]

13. Subtotal: –$1,040 [–$2,340 (#11) + $1,300 (#12)]

14. Depreciation (1st year): $2,900 [MACRS-GDS: $80,000 base divided by 27.5]

15. Taxable Income: –$3,940 [–$1,040 (cash-flow-before-tax minus principal (#13) plus –$2,900 depreciation (#14) to get total taxable income (loss) for 1st year. The result is a loss that shelters your personal income from other sources (#16).]

16. Tax Saving: $1,102 [$3,940 (#15) x .28] [*Smart Tip:* Lowering your income may also lower your "marginal rate" tax bracket, thus reducing tax savings or tax liability. For this reason, some investors believe the cash-flow-before-tax return is a more realistic figure.]

17. Cash Flow Before Tax: –$2,340 [#11]

18. Cash Flow After Tax: –$1,238) [–$2,340 before tax (#11) minus $1,102 tax savings (#16)]

Return After Tax: –4.1% [–$1,230 cash flow after tax (#18) divided by $30,000 cash invested. Note: Depreciation deduction turned a negative cash flow into better return but still negative after tax.]

◆ ◆ ◆

Essential Takeaway: *Smart investors know tax laws and financing options change rapidly, which is why having top-notch advisors is essential to your success. Note that these hypothetical examples are for illustration only and not intended as tax advice. You are strongly encouraged to seek professional consultation from your tax advisor.*

◆ ◆ ◆

STRAIGHT TALK FOR PARENTS

Average room rent (not board) at four-year institutions (public and private) is nearly $5,000 per nine-month school year or about $555/month, according to the National Center for Educational Statistics. That's one big reason why about 8% of second-home buyers in America purchase property to give their college children a place to live, according to the National Association of REALTORS®.

Does buying a place for your kid make sense? Although the answer is "it depends," the right circumstances can turn the answer to a money-making "yes!" Essentially, the answer boils down to whether your children fit — or don't — in your investment equation. Here's why.

● **Talk to your kid.** Not every kid is ready to be a homeowner or property manager. Make sure your offspring is up to the challenge. Being committed to sticking it out at the same school is essential (almost one-third of students transfer colleges once before earning a degree, and nearly 400,000 drop out of college each year). Let's be honest: If this is your student's first time living away from home, he or she may not want this type of parental involvement but would rather be on their own. Consider letting your child spend a year in the dorm — and check out what part of town they want to live in. That market info can be invaluable for parent investors.

● **Cost recovery.** Generally, three years is a short window for appreciation to make up costs of buying, move-in fix-up and especially selling costs, which often run 8%-10% of sale price. *Smart Tip:* One cost-recovery rule of thumb says if you can hold a property until the appreciation increase is as much as your tax bracket, say 28%, then the purchase is worth doing. Bottom line: It takes that much appreciation gain to make up for selling expenses and the lost "free rent" your kid didn't pay.

● **Dorm, rent or buy?** If you're weighing how much it will cost for your scholar's housing, compare the costs of on-campus dorm, off-campus rent and owning a property. After all, no matter the type of student housing, many parents end up paying for it. By letting your kid live there for nothing, your property is giving up the income of one full fair-market rental. Even renting out the extra bedroom(s) doesn't make your offspring's housing free. Conclusion: There's no such thing as free rent.

COLLEGE MATH

On the flip side: If you buy the property all cash, you'll minimize or avoid any mortgage payments. That way one, two or three room rents may cover your operating expenses. Of course, you risk your capital, but with appreciation (hopefully) the investment could pay off. Just remember, it's not a slam dunk if the market is in a slump when you sell. *Smart Tip:* To take advantage of the $250,000 capital gain exemption at sale, the owner (your offspring) will need to be on the deed and/or mortgage and live in the property as their principal residence during any two of the last five years before sale.

● **Depreciation limits.** How you treat the property for tax purposes — as an investment property or second home — has consequences. Again, say your student does not pay rent and manages the property. You pay your scholar's share of rent and rent out the extra bedrooms. Parents pay the expenses and reap the tax benefits. You also cash in on equity buildup and appreciation at sale. Beware of depreciation limits. Because a co-owner (your child) lives in the property but does not pay a "fair market rent," Uncle Sam considers that "personal use," which will be greater than the threshold of 14 days or 10% of total rental days. In that "free rent" scenario, the IRS will not allow you to show a taxable loss from expenses including depreciation. Expenses — including depreciation — may be deducted from income, but not to the point where an actual loss is shown. Thus, if renting out extra bedroom(s) doesn't quite equal expenses, which is possible if you financed the purchase and have a loan payment, then depreciation cannot shelter other income as it would in a fully-rented investment property.

◆ ◆ ◆

Essential Takeaway

Essential Takeaway: *Think of a college property like an investor, not like a parent trying to avoid dorm fees. Buying a kiddie condo or house and paying a mortgage rather than pouring money into a dorm room looks better the longer you hold the property. (1) If your scholar has five or six years of school ahead, or (2) plans to work in the area after school, or (3) if you have serial offspring planning to go to the same school in succession, then the greater-than-three-years' time frame makes the numbers more attractive. Without* *that patient horizon, pay for a dorm or rent instead and enjoy the peace of mind knowing that any change in your kid's plans won't torpedo your investment. One Baby Boomer trend that builds-in a long-term option is (4) if you are considering retiring to the college town yourself someday. Another reason is (5) if you've got season tickets and want to attend games while staying in your own college-town sports condo.*

Once the numbers work on a property, the next step is to buy that goldmine. Here's where your top-notch agent earns the big bucks (paid by seller, of course). But first some essential tips to negotiate a great deal.

HOW TO CRAFT 'WIN-WIN' PURCHASE OFFERS

Smart investors go into negotiations with a "win-win" attitude. Your goal is for both you and the seller to be happy with the deal — not to browbeat the seller into submission. Often, the ability to compromise on one point to get another goes a long way. *Smart Tip:* Owner-occupant sellers may be more emotionally involved with their home and benefit from personal kid-glove treatment. On the other hand, investor sellers are typically interested more in the numbers than the property. Adapt your negotiating approach to appeal to your seller's hot buttons. To get the seller's attention, consider these proven tactics:

▶ Offer a larger than typical earnest-money deposit to show you're serious.

▶ Propose a shorter due-diligence timeframe to get to closing faster.

▶ Be pre-approved for a mortgage or offer all cash to avoid any financing contingency.

▶ An all-cash offer means a flexible closing time frame.

▶ Present your offer in several parts: (1) a Summary Sheet showing the net cash to the seller highlighted in a "bottom line"; (2) a Net Sheet that itemizes how the seller's net proceeds are calculated; and (3) the Contract itself.

CHAPTER 4

COLLEGE MATH

| **Inside Tips On Contingencies And Investment Terms** | All contracts differ, of course, but here are 9 key essentials to consider in every negotiation for income-producing real estate. |

1. Financing Contingency. At the heart of your offer is financing. That's because how you pay for the purchase, especially if seller financing is involved, directly impacts the seller's walk-away cash and your investment return. Include specifics in your contingency, such as total loan amount(s), loan term lengths or dates a second or third mortgage are due (if any), and the particular financing details (for example, down payment of $10,000, which is 10% of purchase price; first mortgage of $45,000 at 5% for 30 years; commercial second mortgage for $20,000 at 6% for 25 years; owner-held third mortgage for $25,000 at 6% interest only for 7 years). *Smart Tip:* Where the purchase involves a loan assumption, include the exact amount of the loan balance, interest rate and remaining loan term so all parties are clear.

2. Inspection Contingency. To be sure the property doesn't have structural or mechanical problems, make the contract contingent on you receiving a satisfactory building inspection report. Typically, the buyer pays for this report. An inspection will either give you peace of mind that all is well or uncover needed repairs that can be negotiated with the seller — or prompt you to walk away.

3. Property Management Contingency. Consider making the contract contingent on the property being accepted by your professional property manager. Often a time limit is included such as 72 hours. This allows your property manager to determine if the property meets market standards and is acceptable for management.

4. Earnest Deposit. Determine local custom; deposits can range from 1.5%-5% of price. Indicate how much money you'll deposit to show your good faith (avoid a token amount), and also the additional amount you plan to add to make up your down payment. Some investors include proof of funds to reassure the seller. This "earnest money" is deposited in escrow and returned to you if the sale does not go through.

5. Due Diligence. This contingency reserves a period between 15 and 60 days depending on the deal's complexity or how much you already know about the market to complete full due diligence and feasibility legwork.

6. **Closing Costs.** The custom of who pays closing fees varies by area, and also shifts between seller's markets and buyer's markets. Consult with your real estate agent and consider asking the seller to pay some or all the closing costs. Giving up this request later during negotiation can smooth the way for acceptance of another point you want to insist upon.

7. **Walk Through.** Unless you agree to accept the property in "as is" condition, the seller is responsible for plumbing, heating, mechanical and electrical systems to be in working order at closing. Include a provision that gives you and/or your investor agent the right to a satisfactory "pre-closing walk-through inspection" no later than the day of closing.

8. **Personal Property.** Essentially, any items that would not cause damage if removed are considered personal property, not real property, and do not convey with the purchase unless itemized in the contract. Don't trust verbal agreements. Be sure to include specific items you want conveyed, such as washer, dryer, refrigerator, slide-in range, light fixtures, drapery rods, chandeliers or other items not physically attached.

9. **Assignment.** Here's where your business partner or mentor may come in, especially if you're learning the business by doing legwork for deals. In the purchaser's line of the contract, you write "[Your Name] and/or Assigns." Also, include an addendum to the effect: "Seller also agrees that this contract is contingent on approval by purchaser's partner." If your partner/mentor puts up the cash to buy, you'll agree on an ownership scenario. Maybe you assign your entire interest or a portion to your partner, or you simply get a finder's fee from the closing proceeds, plus invaluable experience. Whatever you decide, including another legal owner at settlement is convenient and less costly than re-recording the transaction later.

Costly Analysis Mistakes To Avoid

Mistake #1: Not thinking beyond the spreadsheet.

Solution: Beyond the numbers, be sure to determine the progress — if any — toward leasing for the next school year to forecast property income. At all costs, don't be late on the college-town leasing cycle. (More on the lease-up cycle in Chapter 6: LANDLORD U.) Be sure to get all building inspection reports well before the end of the due-diligence period to give you an escape clause if needed to bow out of the deal. Check and recheck your reports and figures to confirm your estimates. If you have doubts — from the property itself to the location to the college-town market — it's better to reconsider before you become the legal owner. *Smart Tip:* If you pass for a grad student or have a college-age-looking associate, you'll be amazed what you can learn from a personal inspection of the property. Making it clear upfront that you're not a cop will help the kids open up. Want to know about bad plumbing, roof leaks, unreliable cable/Internet, competing rent rates, parking permits or deferred maintenance? They'll tell you. After all, you may be their landlord someday.

Mistake #2: Not distinguishing between minor and major problems.

Solutions: When building inspections turn up small or minor problems, they can be negotiated with a minor price adjustment. If the problems are major — or the seller is hiding them — better to walk away from the deal. Even large price reductions rarely are enough to pay for the hidden problems that could surface after your signature dries. Remember: Most real estate investments don't turn out exactly as forecast. Twists, turns and the unexpected can throw a curve into your math — but running the numbers is an essential starting point. Refining the estimates comes later when the real income and expenses hit the fan. *Smart Tip:* Don't rely on your lender's approval to certify that a property is a good deal. Lenders want to lend money not triple check whether your cost estimates are too high, your rent too low, your vacancy/occupancy projections are history-based — or any of the zillion mistaken assumptions or projections that can make a rental property a dumb deal. Do your own legwork and double check your numbers.

Rely on your agent. Take your time. Sweat the small stuff at the numbers and negotiation stage. Ultimately, you'll pull the trigger and buy some property. Knowing how you'll pay for the property is essential — and the subject of the next chapter on FINANCIAL AID.

Chapter 4 Roundup

Smart Essentials COLLEGE MATH ::
What You Have Learned

▶▶ How to analyze a goldmine when you find one.

▶▶ 5 key assumptions that impact your numbers.

▶▶ 4 essential numbers to run a smart property analysis.

    Number #1: Price-To-Rent

    Number #2: Cash-On-Cash Return

    Number #3: Internal Rate Of Return

    Number #4: Cash Flow Before And After Taxes

▶▶ Straight talk for college parents.

▶▶ How to craft 'win-win' purchase offers.

▶▶ Inside tips on contingencies and investment terms.

▶▶ Costly analysis mistakes to avoid.

FINANCIAL AID

In this chapter, you will learn smart ways to:

1. **Find the cash you need to be a player in college-rental investments.**

2. **Discover inside tips to buy with 'Other People's Money.'**

3. **Pick the investor financing strategy that fits your needs like a golden glove.**

The market is right. The property fits. The deal is coming together. Now paying for your property is where the rubber meets the road.

To close your college-town real estate deal requires (1) a down payment ("equity"), (2) financing (if you don't buy all cash), and (3) management (we'll get to that shortly in Chapter 6: LANDLORD U).

SMART WAYS TO FIND CASH FOR YOUR PURCHASE

As a parent or investor, assembling your down payment equity is Job One. Essentially, if you plan to be "one and done" buying only one rental—think college parents—then putting as much cash into the deal as possible makes sense. More equity reduces the expense of mortgage financing and gives you maximum cash flow as well as a cushion for the unexpected. If, on the other hand, you plan to buy multiple properties—think serious investor—making 20%-25% down payments and conserving your "hard money" cash equity for future deals is smart.

Where Does The Money Come From? Start with personal money. Savings, cash-out refi on your principal home or taking a home equity loan or home equity line of credit (see "self-financing" strategy) are smart starts. Some parents and investors borrow from brokerage accounts or take loans against paid-in cash from a whole-life insurance policy. Multi-property investors sometimes assemble partners who put up cash. In the partnership approach, typically you ("operating partner") find the property, run the numbers, line up financing and pitch the deal to your "limited" partners. If they (or your mentor) turn the deal down, then either the numbers don't work (cash flow is too optimistic or expenses and reserves are not conservative enough) or the property is a mistake (location not close-in, vacancy/occupancy iffy, deferred repairs, etc.). *Smart Tip:* Walk away if the deal doesn't cut the muster with your partners. Really big-time investors move up from joint ventures (active partners share cash flow and appreciation) to larger equity pools, such as big money syndications (silent money partners in regulated offering) or institutional partners (big-league multi-million-dollar deals).

Expect to pay more. Once your cash equity is in place, then lining up financing is next. With today's interest rates and attractive loan programs available on investment real estate, now is a perfect time to buy rental property. Be aware, though, lenders ask for larger down payments and charge somewhat higher interest rates for mortgages on non-owner-occupied properties. There's good reason.

Lenders consider investment property a higher risk than financing owner-occupied homes because investors have less to lose than owners walking away from a home they live in. There's also a greater risk the investor could default if the property sits vacant for a long period. Let's be honest: Investors who rely on rental income to make the monthly payment can quickly run into trouble. In addition, some renters don't care for properties as well as a live-in owner — which over time can erode the property's value. For all the above reasons, lenders may require personal loan guarantees[tt] ("recourse financing") from investors.

> [tt] *Personal Loan Guarantees*
> Some lenders require investors to personally guarantee any shortfall at loan pay off. If property values drop, owners can be "underwater" at sale because the property is worth less than the outstanding loan amount. The lender's recourse is to make the borrower pay the deficiency. *Smart Tip:* Look hard for a non-recourse lender that doesn't require a personal loan guarantee, with the exception of standard carve-outs for fraud or transfer without approval. A successful investor track record helps. If you must sign a guarantee, run your cash flow and reserve numbers carefully, vet them with a third party (mentor, accountant, other investor) and put down enough cash to make a loan-payoff-deficiency unlikely at sale. Peace of mind is a wonderful thing.

FINANCIAL AID

8 STRATEGIES TO BUY RENTALS WITH 'OTHER PEOPLE'S MONEY'

This section shares smart strategies for covering purchase costs when you buy rental property. Choosing the "best" financing method depends as much on your circumstances as on the property and lenders' requirements. Numerous computer apps make it easy to compare terms and costs across different loan structures. Ask your lender, real estate agent, accountant or mentor for software or website recommendations.

● Strategy #1: All Cash

For parents and investors with deep pockets — or for low-cost bargain properties — buying all cash maximizes your cash-flow income. Variations include a large down payment, say, 50% or more, that reduces mortgage expenses for interest and principal. The NAR reports that about half of all investor buyers pay all cash. On a $100,000 property, the purchaser pays $100,000 all cash. No financing is required. The all-cash strategy has the benefit of avoiding lender's red tape and having to consult partners (if any) for every decision. The downside is you need to have the funds personally, and you're risking your money, not other people's money.

Benefits: Sellers know the deal will close smoothly, and they will walk away with cash in hand. That confidence can make some sellers open to a price concession, where an offer from a buyer who needs financing may be less attractive even at full price.

● Strategy #2: Self-Financing

If you don't have enough cash sitting around, a time-honored strategy is to self-finance the purchase with an equity loan, home equity line of credit (HELOC) or cash-out refi on your home for the cash payment and rehab expenses. Equity financing means you have original cash equity, sweat equity and appreciation on your side.

Benefits: Self-financing avoids applying to the bank for purchase financing. Rental income will repay the amount taken from the credit line, or you can repay the line when you sell. Both approaches leave your credit line available for additional investments.

● Strategy #3: Owner-Occupied Financing

Investments typically are property that the borrower does not occupy. Lenders treat investment properties as higher risk, charging higher interest rates and closing fees. If the property, however, is for your kid, you may qualify for a lower-cost "owner-occupied mortgage." Ask your lender about special financing to buy homes for a college-bound child. *Without* this financing, transactions are often considered "investment properties" with higher rates and costs. *With* the financing, the loan can be treated as a vacation or second-home mortgage. Here's the rub: If the borrower or the property doesn't meet the lender's rules (requirements vary), the property may be treated as an investment property.

FHA lender requirements for owner-occupied loan with parents co-signing:

▶ Child must prove college enrollment.

▶ Child must be a co-borrower on the mortgage.

▶ Property must be a single-family residence, not a multi-family building.

▶ Property must be located close to the college where the student is enrolled.

▶ If a condo, then condominium development must be an FHA-approved community.

▶ Child must occupy the property for a minimum of one year and property cannot be rented, although housemates are permitted.

▶ Parents cannot own other investment properties or a second/ vacation home in the same location as the student's home.

▶ Parents' credit and income (the child's income is not included), plus the child's credit score are used to qualify for the loan. (The child's debts, collection accounts, etc. could disqualify the loan). If the child is old enough, the child is the primary borrower (owner occupant) and the co-signing parents are co-borrowers (owner non-occupants).

Be warned: Lenders can inspect to make sure the borrowers actually live in the property. Worst case: If the borrower (your scholar) doesn't live there, the lender can demand that the note (mortgage) be paid immediately or can prosecute you. Mortgage fraud is serious, and falsely stating the borrower intends to occupy a college property tops the list.

Establish State Residency To Save Big On In-State Tuition And Financing

Being a property owner and being responsible for mortgage payments can be essential for your scholar to meet residency qualifications. Expect school rules, an application and deadlines.

It's not uncommon to require one year of living in the state (freshman year), one full year of declaring an intention to become a resident (file application early), financial independence (being on a deed and mortgage helps). Bottom line: Residency requirements vary by state and institution. Ask your attorney or real estate agent for state and local rules where you're buying a college rental property.

Smart Tip: Putting your offspring on the deed can save in two ways: (1) Establish state residency for lower in-state tuition (essential for out-of-state parents); (2) Save on lower property taxes as an owner-occupied principal residence rather than an investment property. If you are buying in-state, you may only want your offspring to co-sign the mortgage as an "owner-occupied second home" for financing reasons. Ask your lender and real estate agent for details.

● Strategy #4: 25/75 Investor Financing

With a fixed-rate mortgage, either conventional or government-backed, you borrow up to 75% of the purchase price at a flat interest rate for a fixed term, often 25 or 30 years. Your monthly principal and interest payments remain level throughout the mortgage (taxes, insurance and other fees can increase). You pay 25% down and finance 75% loan-to-value (LTV) with a commercial loan.

Benefits: You pay 25% down and get the best market financing. Also a 25% down payment drives up your cash-on-cash return. *Smart Tip:* If you make a down payment of less than 20%, (1) it may carry a higher interest rate and (2) it may require you to purchase private mortgage insurance (PMI) to protect the lender from default because you have less skin in the game than 20%. Find a way to get an 80% LTV loan and use a secondary financing source, such as a credit line, for the 20% down payment. That way you minimize your out-of-pocket expense plus lower your monthly payment by eliminating PMI. Use seller concessions to keep upfront cash for closing/settlement costs low.

● Strategy #5: FHA 'Kiddie Condo' Loans

FHA financing is possible for parents to buy property for college-bound kids. Often referred to as "Kiddie Condo" loans, FHA allows "non-occupant co-borrower" loans to close as owner-occupied mortgages. FHA doesn't actually make loans, rather it insures loans ("government-backed loans") which makes commercial lenders willing to finance rental properties at lower interest rates and with a lower down payment. When you put less than 20% down, FHA requires a mortgage insurance premium (MIP), what a conventional lender calls private mortgage insurance (PMI). New rules went into effect in 2013 that require MIP to be paid for 11 years (or the term of the loan, whichever comes first) if the original loan-to-value (LTV) ratio is between 80%–90% LTV (excluding any up-front MIP that is financed). On mortgages initiated with LTV higher than 90%, the MIP must be paid for the life of the loan (or 30 years, whichever comes first). FHA knows the occupant will not make the mortgage payment; instead, the parents who do not occupy the home will. As of this writing, FHA allows these loans if the property is a one-unit home, the co-borrower is a blood relative (parent, grandparent, sibling, etc.) who qualifies for the loan using their income or assets, and the seller of the home is not related to the buyer or the non-occupant co-borrower. Both borrowers take title to the property and sign for the loan. (Ask your lender for any rule changes.)

'Kiddie Condo' loan advantages:

▶ A student can use a blood-relative's cash and credit to qualify.

▶ Property qualifies for all primary-residence tax advantages because it's "owner occupied."

▶ Renting space to roommates is allowed.

▶ A low down payment compared with other financing options.

▶ A lower, owner-occupied interest rate on the mortgage versus higher investment-property interest rate.

▶ Helps the college student establish a solid credit rating.

▶ Tax benefits, such as deducting mortgage interest and real estate taxes, can be divided among owners, according to who pays the expense. See your tax advisor for details.

▶ FHA loans are assumable (with FHA approval), which means your buyer could inherit your low interest rate—a definite marketing advantage if interest rates go up between your purchase and sale.

Smart Tip: The property does not have to be a condo. If it is a condo, then the parent-investor needs to make sure the project is FHA-approved or that the property can get a "spot approval."

Benefits: FHA "Kiddie Condo" financing is specifically tailored for parents, especially in today's market, to make college affordable and to encourage converting residential foreclosures into rentals. With this financing, there is no need for the seller to take back a loan note and resale homes (not new construction) are typical.

● Strategy #6: Adjustable-Rate Mortgage (ARM)

Doesn't that low rate look great? Here's the catch. ARMs have a fixed repayment period, say 30 years, but the interest changes — and thus payments change — on a periodic schedule based on a particular interest index, such as Treasury Bills. ARMs usually have adjustment period and lifetime maximums on rate increases. ARMs are best for investors that want maximum income in the early years, but they aren't for everybody. The downside is that ARMs will adjust on a preset schedule, for example, payments are fixed for 5 or 7 initial years, then adjust annually for the remainder of the loan. The risk is that rate/payment adjustments may cause higher expenses later but rents may not be equally adjustable. Although maximum increases of interest and payment are capped for each adjustment period and also over the life of the loan, the unknown cost may not be acceptable for "buy and hold" investors.

Benefits: In the first years, ARMs can produce maximum positive cash flow with low monthly loan payments, which can give you the highest possible income before taxes. That's why ARMs make sense for investors with a short-hold horizon of fewer than five years — such as parents with graduation in sight.

● Strategy #7: Reverse Mortgage

If you are 62+ and have home equity, a don't-pay-till-later reverse mortgage is a consideration for investment property. Too good to be true? Almost. Compare costs carefully, and weigh taking money from an equity loan or cash-out refi instead. Fees for reverse mortgages can be buzz killers. Upfront fees can include origination, points, mortgage insurance premiums, closing costs, servicing fees. Interest is generally not deductible unless you make prepayments on the loan. Backend fees at sale of your home can also zap profits (assuming you care because you're not dead), such as admin fees or the lender takes a share of original equity at time of loan ("maturity fees") or the lender takes a share of the home's price increase since the mortgage date ("appreciation fees").

Benefits: These loans are sometimes called "grandparent" financing, for relatives with more equity than current income because with a reverse mortgage, you don't make any monthly loan payments. There are no restrictions on how you spend the money. The loan is paid back when the house sells or the owner dies ("maturity event").

💬 Strategy #8: Fannie Mae Dedicated Student Housing Loan Program

This Fannie Mae program is specifically for large investors and is run through a nationwide network of Delegated Underwriting and Servicing (DUS) approved lenders who make loans of $1 million or more for dwellings containing 5 or more units. These loans are specifically designed to offer affordable permanent financing for dedicated student housing. Maximums include: 75% loan to value, 25-year term and amortization. Even if your plans aren't in this Big League, it's instructive to see how Fannie Mae defines eligible properties:

▶ Must be dedicated student housing with a resident student concentration of over 80%.

▶ Property must be located within two miles of the campus or on a university-sanctioned bus line.

▶ 12-month lease terms are required with either a parental guarantee or personal guarantee by gainfully employed students.

▶ University enrollment must be at least 10,000 students with the majority being full-time.

▶ Properties must have sufficient security.

▶ Food service is not allowed.

▶ "By the bed" income calculation is permitted as long as it is comparable to similar student properties or if there is successful history of such accounting.

Benefits: These loans are specifically targeted to dedicated student housing and larger properties. Various rates and terms are available from approved DUS lenders—list available at *http://www.FannieMae.com.*

◆ ◆ ◆

Essential Takeaway: Regardless whether you invest individually or through a partnership, investors use financing to leverage the number or size of holdings or vary down payments to maximize cash flow. In today's financing maze, there are five smart essentials for success: (1) Maximize your credit score. A score below 740 can cost you in higher rates or require paying points to buy down the rate to be affordable. Check your

credit early to be prepared. (2) Make a sizable down payment. You'll get the best interest rate at 25% down or more, if you can swing it. (3) Don't be afraid to ask owners if they would consider seller financing. With the uptick in motivated sellers wanting to get rid of their properties, more owners will consider helping you with the financing. Be sure to have a blueprint for the terms and figures you want. (4) Consider a partnership or private loan (also "hard money") from an individual who wants to own real estate but lacks time or know-how to find, purchase and manage property. (5) Don't say you'll live in the property when you won't. There are laws against scams using "straw buyers."

◆ ◆ ◆

Keep reading to learn more of the essential ins and outs of being a student-housing investor the smart way in the next chapter: LANDLORD U.

Chapter 5 Roundup

**Smart Essentials FINANCIAL AID ::
What You Have Learned**

▶▶ Smart ways to find cash for your purchase.
▶▶ 8 strategies to buy rentals with 'other people's money.'
 ▶ *Strategy #1:* All Cash
 ▶ *Strategy #2:* Self-Financing
 ▶ *Strategy #3:* Owner-Occupied Financing
 ▶ *Strategy #4:* 25/75 Investor Financing
 ▶ *Strategy #5:* FHA 'Kiddie Condo' Loan
 ▶ *Strategy #6:* Adjustable Rate Mortgage (ARM)
 ▶ *Strategy #7:* Reverse Mortgage
 ▶ *Strategy #8:* Fannie Mae Dedicated Student
  Housing Loan Program

Smart Essentials

Page	Essential Note

LANDLORD U

In this chapter, you'll learn smart ways to:

1. Master the student-housing calendar to your advantage.

2. Avoid all-too-common housing discrimination mistakes.

3. Know everything you need to manage student rentals.

STUDENTS LIVE LIKE SLOBS AND PARTY LIKE ANIMALS. SO WHAT'S NEW?

There it's said. If one is not to despair over the future of America, don't inspect student apartments. Seriously, if stained carpet, rooms full of beer cans (literally), busted drywall hidden by shocking posters, amazing collections of shot glasses, beer bottles or hot sauces, gear spread around like a tornado tore through it, pilfered signage and students still zonked in bed at noon (sometimes with someone else) or if resident pizza boxes (partially empty) will make you sorry you ever invested in college real estate, then reconsider. If through all the above—and then some— you can roll with the territory all the way to the bank, read on.

Get Your Master's Degree In Residential Life

Students are experts in student life, especially housing. You must be too. Although it varies from town to town, the most organized students start thinking about next year's housing after Christmas break— and sometimes even before Thanksgiving! Study the school's website. Most universities offer students a 12-month dorm lease that begins with the fall term (August) or at the end of the previous school year (May). Give special note to this campus-housing lifecycle. Typically, in February or March, there is a deadline for applications (and deposits) for fall semester. Applications are often prioritized in the order submitted. Sometime later is the notification deadline when students find out if they got their choice or got any housing at all.

This notification deadline is critical for you. The bad news releases a deluge of disappointed students looking for off-campus digs. Some schools have websites, housing fairs and special services to help students connect with off-campus landlords. The next wave in the housing timeline comes from on-campus students who change their minds or whose plans change (particularly roommate plans). If you haven't rented for the entire next school year by late spring, this second wave, often in late spring or early summer, is a meager lifeline. Finally, a wavelet of last-minute admissions and transfers hits the streets in August or September, just before classes begin. Ideally college landlords don't wait for this final trickle of tenant prospects.

Often, tenant turnover months are May or August. Picture thousands of apartments emptied and repaired to be ready for move-in within days — and construction and cleaning crews racing to the next building to repeat the drill in overtime. Whatever the rhythm of rentals in your market, you'll need to master that local calendar — or risk budget-busting vacancies. *Smart Tip:* If you are buying a property, be sure to find out where the old landlord stands in the lease-up process for next year. Avoid the worst case where you close on the property without tenants after the local lease-up period has ended. Once most students have gone home, you may snag a few stragglers but you'll want to adjust your revenue forecast — and perhaps your offer price — downward for that year.

◆ ◆ ◆

Essential Takeaway: Although student leases may run from August through July or June through May, college landlords often require payment in advance for summer months at the beginning or end of the lease year. Prepaid rent insures tenants pay before they move in and get a key. Prepayment also makes sure the landlord is paid for the summer months when many students skip town. That puts the burden to sublet on the tenant, not a burden on the landlord's vacancy losses. Ask your real estate agent or property manager for local custom, which varies widely from one college town to another.

◆ ◆ ◆

TOP 10 SMART WAYS TO FIND STUDENT TENANTS

No matter whether you advertise early when students are looking—or leave it to just before the current lease ends—here's how to find renters for your property.

1. Craigslist and Backpage (free and ubiquitous; learn how to refresh your listing to move it back on top.)

2. Post or advertise rental listings online: Search: "[school name] off-campus housing" and you'll find tons of sites: LiveOffCampus.com, CollegeProwler.com, GoOffCampus.com, Placefinder.com, uLoop.com, Walkscore.com, Rent.com, ForRent.com, etc. (Develop a simple website for your property with photos and details you can update yourself.)

3. Word of mouth, especially among roommates.

4. Student newspaper and digital-edition classifieds.

5. Bulletin boards, message pillars and community kiosks. (You sometimes find these within specific schools, facilities or hospital departments.)

6. Off-campus housing fairs and listing services provided by the university. (Meet the person in the housing office responsible for working with local landlords.)

7. Signage on unit, property or nearby traffic thoroughfares. (Local sign ordinances may apply.)

8. Referrals from other landlords, particularly same-type properties that are already rented. ("I'll help you if you help me.")

9. Register property with the school's housing office as student or staff housing. (This landlord list is also handy to identify other local student housing owners.)

10. List your rental with real estate and management companies. (Typically requires you pay a rental commission.)

A Word About Federal, State And Local Landlord-Tenant Laws

As a landlord, you'll be responsible for following housing and landlord-tenant laws (ignorance is no excuse). Federal law covers lead paint and asbestos, and nationwide rules are set by the

Civil Rights Act, Fair Housing Act, Americans With Disabilities Act, and Fair Credit Reporting Act. State law typically regulates rent-increase notices, security deposits, right-of-entry for landlord, housing standards, rental rules, repairs and maintenance and evictions. Local ordinances cover much the same legal landscape, but tend to put a finer point on building codes, health and safety issues, evictions, etc.

Here are some issues that may — or may not — be ruled by your local laws:

▶ Does local law provide for additional "protected groups" for fair housing beyond federal law, such as occupation, income source, immigration status, elderliness (55+), sexual orientation, etc.?

▶ Are landlords forced to remodel for handicap access — or allow the tenant to remodel?

▶ Can landlords charge an application fee, and can they keep all or some of the application fee or must they return the entire fee to a rejected renter?

▶ Is the landlord allowed to collect the last month or two of rent in advance?

▶ Must the landlord give dated receipts for each rent payment?

▶ When can landlords keep or must they return security/damage deposits?

▶ Do local rules require landlords to put deposits in interest-bearing escrow accounts and pay tenants accrued interest at lease end?

▶ Must landlords offer first right of refusal to renters if the building is to be sold?

▶ Is it illegal locally to convert attics or basements into rental units, or turn a single-family home into a multi-unit rental?

▶ Are there Fair Housing Act exemptions for landlords who rent only one, two or three units or bedrooms in their own homes?

▶ Do local rent-control rules apply to your building?

▶ Does your area require window guards, door peepscopes, recycling of newspaper, glass, plastic, aluminum, removal of lead paint?

▶ Are local landlords required to supply screens, storm windows or blinds?

▶ Do tenants have the right to stop paying rent if the landlord doesn't make needed repairs?

◆ ◆ ◆

Essential Takeaway: *Get a good, local landlord-tenant lawyer on your team early. Not only will you want to comply with all local, state and federal laws from the get-go, you'll also want the lawyer to review your lease and maybe your advertising, tenant screening and record keeping. Be sure to have a written agreement of lawyer's fees and expectations. To find a legal specialist, ask your mentor, investor network, landlord association or local housing authority.*

◆ ◆ ◆

What Landlords Must Know About Housing Discrimination In Renter Ads

To be a smart landlord, you must understand the federal, state and local laws against discriminating against "protected groups" when advertising, interviewing and selecting renters.

When it comes to advertising, including written and oral statements and pictures, federal Fair Housing rules forbid indicating a preference, limitations or discrimination based on race, color, sex, national origin, family status (married, single, divorced or number of children), disabilities or religion. What's more, you can't use publications or other media that are accessible only to limited groups.

What does this mean in a landlord's world?

Describe the property, not the people. Focus on the property and its features, not the background of tenants. Avoid some of these doozies that have been ruled discriminatory:

▶ "Please no undergraduates. Professionals and graduate students only."

▶ "Desirable for Spanish-speaking individual"

▶ "Perfect for working females"

▶ "Walking distance to mosque"

▶ "Handicapped welcome"

▶ "Membership approval required"

▶ "Fraternity men need not apply"

- ▶ "Charming old-world Polish neighborhood"
- ▶ "Adult building, no children"
- ▶ "No drinkers, smokers"
- ▶ "Not suitable for disabled, physically fit only"
- ▶ "Female roommate," "male housemate" terms discriminate for an individual unit, but may be okay relating to shared living quarters.

MORE STRAIGHT TALK FOR PARENTS

Many parents quickly make the leap: "And with Johnny living there, he can help collect rents and manage the property." They envision their scholar learning about real estate and business before their classmates. Some parents imagine how sharing the common enterprise with their kid will bring them closer.

Whoa, Nellie.

It's one thing for an 18- to 24-year-old to be your tenant—it's quite another for them to be your property manager—not to mention your business partner. Here's why.

Does Having Your Kid Be Your Property Manager Make Sense?

Let's face it: Not every college kid is ready to be a responsible property manager. All it takes is some uncollected rent, one argument with roommates or a wild party to expose the weakness in having your kid be your property manager. Think hard—and talk with your kid—about expecting them to live in and manage your property. For many young people, college is a first time away from home, meant for discovery and to reinvent themselves, rather than have a second job managing their parents' real estate. Yes, students need to learn how to be self-supporting. But parents at some point need to let go and let kids be, even if it's not ideal for the parent's investment.

🗨 **Junior manager.** Consider involving the kid in a limited fashion — maintenance (vacuuming stairs, shoveling snow, mowing yard) or being the first contact to assess repair needs before calling property management or being the ambassador to other tenants are possibilities. If you don't trust your child to keep up his or her own unit (compare their bedroom) and set the tone for others, then think again about offering any property responsibility.

Personality. Another assessment parents should make, besides maturity, is the general personality of their offspring. Some people hate living without others around. Other scholars thrive on being alone with fewer distractions. For these offspring, a cheap rental studio may be a better fit than being "Director of Wildlife Management," as our dean of students at Beloit College described his job. Knowing the ins and outs of a student's personality can be essential. *Smart Tip:* Gauge your kid's interest level by taking him/her along on the home shopping tour with your agent. If you see interest scouting places, then maybe real estate property management is an option.

Freedom. Another point that bears repeating: Some students want to live on campus, go Greek or change their minds—quit, drop out, transfer, go abroad, finish in record time or take a gap year before grad school, you name it. Include your child's perspective before pulling the trigger to buy a student rental that assumes they're the manager. Parent landlords should ask themselves: If your kid walked away from the rental, would your investment plans be devastated? If so, then reconsider being a college-parent landlord. If not, then full steam ahead.

Post-grads. Post-graduates are a different animal from undergraduate students. Graduate students are often older, more seasoned, more focused on keeping their costs down now that they are paying for themselves rather than pile on the alternative: more student-loan debt. Some are married with families. Others expect to stay near the university for three to six years, especially those requiring residencies, internships and post-grad dissertations. Still others may become employed by the university after graduation. If your offspring fit this scenario, maybe they are suited to be your partner.

◆ ◆ ◆

Essential Takeaway

Essential Takeaway: Don't pin your investment prospects and your College Math on having your offspring manage the property. If you do not plan to personally manage the property, hire a professional property manager. In the event your kid takes an interest and shows an aptitude to learn about real estate and investing, then that's a plus. But expecting your kid to be your business partner is most often not a smart plan for either of you.

◆ ◆ ◆

Why Hire A Professional Property Manager? There are a unique set of headaches to off-campus housing: (1) rowdy renters tend to upset neighbors, (2) students can be rough on property, (3) rent collection from students can be difficult, (4) college-town housing tends to be management-intensive (time is money), (5) college policies on student enrollment and housing can change, and, (6) forecasting shifting student demand can be tricky. *Smart Tip:* Learn from the pros. Talk with your top agent or your mentor or local landlords that gather in an investor's club. Check for student complaints registered with the housing office. Find out who delivers great property management — and what it includes and costs (tenant acquisition, repairs/maintenance, rent collection, financial reports, etc.). In the long run, good service at higher fees trumps bad service at lower fees. If you find your own renters and all you need is someone to maintain the property, an eager-to-please small operator can be better than the biggest in town. Also, having a list of reliable service providers — plumber, electrician, carpenter, handyman, etc. — that you and your offspring/manager can turn to may be sufficient.

Compared with other rental markets, college-town student housing has an extraordinarily short lease-up window . . . unlike in-fill leases rolling throughout the year. To ensure all your rental beds are full in the fall, you will need to concentrate efforts before the spring leasing season. To lease and manage a rental, a great property manager needs to fish upstream for renters, advertising and marketing for renters before renters are needed. Find out what a prospective property manager does that's exceptional to guarantee maximum occupancy. Some tell-tale signs include a property website with photos, maps, advantages; referral bounty system; active social media presence; frequent Craigslist/Backpage and other online postings; ad tracking to separate what works from what doesn't. You'll spot a clever lease manager when you meet one . . . and he or she will have the track record to prove it. Hire that manager.

How Much Do You Charge For Wear And Tear And Damage Deposits? Yes, some college tenants major in partying more than studying, and may punch holes in drywall and spill stuff on carpets or just be irresponsible. Keep in mind — and in your budget — that wear and tear from normal comings and goings is not covered by security deposits. Why is that important? It means you must be prepared to steam-clean or rip out the carpet and paint at least every two years — and maybe between every set of tenants.

The advantage of student housing is that you always have a constant stream of tenants. The disadvantage is that you always have a constant stream of tenants.

Student-housing security deposits. Ask other landlords, other investors, what they charge for damage deposits. It is not uncommon for student housing deposits to be large because of the damage students can cause. Be clear what is included (use move-in and move-out checklists with photos — especially dispute-prone items such as oven, fridge, toilets — that all parties sign and date after a walk-through orientation). Some student-housing landlords separate into multiple deposits: one to protect against tenants walking away before the lease is up (rental loss), another for damages, particularly more costly repairs such as appliances, doors, cabinets, fixtures, and another "regular" security deposit for minor damage that is greater than normal wear and tear. Be sure you check with your rental attorney to confirm that no local ordinances forbid multiple or large deposits greater than one rent payment. Deposit money legally belongs to the renter unless the landlord has a valid claim, and must be returned within a reasonable time after lease end. *Smart Tip:* When using a standard lease, be sure your tenants understand upfront that regardless who caused the damage (or disappeared without paying their rent), everyone named on the lease is responsible for covering the cost. Having parents co-sign ("parental guarantees") as one entity can be an insurance policy of recourse.

Furnished Or Unfurnished?

Renting furnished or unfurnished varies by college-town custom. Completely or partially furnishing the unit(s) can help target specific tenant groups, especially higher income faculty, visiting or adjunct professors and summer renters. Furnishings also give your units an edge over the competition. If you do go the furnished route, consider providing the "big basics": refrigerator/freezer, stove, washer/dryer, appliances, kitchen cookware or "furnished kitchen," dining and coffee tables, chairs, beds, dressers, sofas, desks, bookshelves, curtains or blinds, etc. Another technique to make your property stand out is to offer broadband with "high-speed

Internet, cable, secure Wi-Fi and landline" or include other utilities. Consider tenant-paid heat and A/C to encourage moderate use. Let tenants provide the IKEA things: linens, tableware, dishes, lamps, TVs, etc. *Smart Tip:* Consider a separate furnishings damage deposit. Set aside a furniture replacement reserve.

Lease Restrictions That May Be Important To You

College leases are as unique as every property and every investor. Beyond the "boiler plate" basics, be sure to have your lease reviewed by an experienced local attorney who specializes in real estate law. Not only does a lease or agreement specify the terms and conditions but it also gives you legal basis to enforce rental policies.

Common issues:

▶ **Advance rent:** Collect first and last month, or summer rents against tenant leaving without notice, plus a security deposit.

▶ **House rules:** Smoking, keys, property care, appliance use, noise, waterbeds, overnight visitors becoming co-tenants, maximum occupants, etc.

▶ **Lease change:** The process to make mutually agreeable changes to lease in writing.

▶ **Lease period:** 10 or 12 months? Longer? Renewal procedure, deadline?

▶ **Maintenance:** Any tasks required of tenant, such as snow removal, lawn care or put out garbage for pickup.

▶ **Parking:** Restrictions on vehicles—number, type, parking location (such as not on lawn).

▶ **Payment:** Will you accept check, money order, cash, online or PayPal-like account? Parental guarantee?

▶ **Penalties:** Late payment fee definition—how much, bounced check penalty, attorney's fees paid by tenant.

▶ **Pets:** Allowed? If so, weight limit or acceptable breeds and total number. Pet deposit?

▶ **Repairs:** Should renters pay first $25 or $50?

▶ **Security deposit:** How much? Rules for applying deposit to repairs and refund.

▶ **Sub-letting:** Forbidden or "subletting with permission not to be unreasonably withheld"? If so, notification or lease change required?

▶ **Termination:** Amount of notice to terminate and termination triggers.

▶ **Utilities:** Landlord or tenant name on accounts. Who pays water/gas/sewer separate from electricity? Payment included in rent?

▶ **Vacate notice:** Date required and penalty if "late" notice.

Costly College-Housing Management Mistakes To Avoid

Mistake #1: Getting your bottom-line blown away by mid-term turnover.
Roommates squabble. Students come and go. They drop out. They get kicked out. They transfer. They graduate. That's the nature of college. This turnover can be costly, especially if it hits you in mid-term and new renters are hard to find. One solution is to build in a referral and bounty system into your lease. Simply let tenants know that you will reward them for word-of-mouth roommate finding with, say, half a month's rent credit (same price a real estate agent charges to find a renter), if they find a replacement roommate and there is no rent gap. Be sure to vet the new roommates for credit and get every renter to sign your lease or rental agreement.

Mistake #2: Losing one-quarter of your rental income to summer vacancies.
Lost rent for two or three months can be the iceberg to your Titanic cash-flow projections. Lease for 12 months, not the 9- or 10-month school-year term. Some landlords promote a "back to school" special in the spring. A lease term that runs from June to May (not September to May) is effective to lock-in renters early, especially if you allow subletting for summer or permission to store possessions over the summer. Flexibility is key. Be sure to make all lease signers responsible for rent payment.

Mistake #3: Falling prey to 'Animal House' syndrome.
Do you remember how students treated property when you were in school? Ouch. Who would ever want to be a student landlord? Our glib but truthful answer is: Don't rent to the animals in the first place.

You can avoid the kids majoring in Partying 101 with high-quality tenant screening. Require references from previous landlords and credit-check all tenants, not just the lead renter. Faced with multiple applications, there's nothing to prevent you from preferring medical students or graduate students that study more than they party. Also, where possible, install hardware and fixtures designed to withstand hard use (metal doors, synthetic carpet, Formica counters, sturdy appliances, shower enclosures, surplus-capacity electric wiring, etc.). Hefty security/damage deposits are wise. Also, get parents or guardians to co-sign the lease or rental agreement and be legally and financially responsible for their kid's behavior. Keep tabs on the property throughout the year, not just when the rent check is late. *Smart Tip:* Even with responsible tenants, be sure to reserve funds for improvements and replacements. Consider setting up a capital account at purchase, designed to pay for unexpected repairs and emergencies. Contribute to that account annually to prepare for scheduled replacements.

Mistake #4: Not solving the problem of student tenants with no credit or income.
What is a landlord to do with applicants who have no income, no credit history, or little rental record? Here are some solutions: (1) Check with the university for dorm behavior or if the student is behind on payments to the school. (Get permission to check from the prospective tenant.) Consider asking for an advance rent payment or larger deposit if problems are found. (2) Have a parent or guardian co-sign the lease (a must if the applicant is under 18) to guarantee payment of their child's share. (3) Lease the place by the unit not by the bed. Make all tenants as a group joint-and-severally liable to pay the whole rent, utilities (if not included) and damages, not just their bedroom share. Yes, large developers mostly rent by the bed. But they have the staff to fill the beds one by one, refill empty beds mid-year, manage all the individual leases and collect many more rent payments. For the small landlord, having parental co-signers and rent by the unit is simpler.

| **Last Word** | As a veteran college-town investor once said, "Goldmines are created by good management. Bad management creates a mine disaster." |

Next stop: GRADUATION. Know how to cash out when the time is right.

Chapter 6 Roundup

Smart Essentials LANDLORD U ::
What You Have Learned

▶▶ Students live like slobs and party like animals.
So what's new?
▶▶ Top 10 smart ways to find student tenants.
▶▶ What landlords must know about anti-discrimination rules.
▶▶ Making your kid your property manager could work —
or not.
▶▶ When hiring a professional property manager is worth
the money.
▶▶ Lease restrictions that may be important to you.
▶▶ Costly college-housing management mistakes to avoid.

Smart Essentials

Page   **Essential Note**

CHAPTER 7
GRADUATION

In this chapter, you will learn smart ways to:

1. Time the right moment to cash out your investment.

2. Use equity buildup to trigger your profit-taking strategies.

3. Select from five ways to cash out that fit your investment goals.

SMART WAYS TO TIME YOUR MARKET EXIT

The best time to sell an investment property is when you're ready. That said: There are some better times than others in every market — especially the college-town housing market. Tune in to the pulse of your market and it will tell you the right time. Often the ideal time to sell is later fall or winter. Why? You want to close in advance of the leasing open season so that new investors — like you — have time to run numbers and fill vacancies.

As an investor seller, your property is most attractive with paying tenants under lease. As a parent seller, you're likely to put your investment on the market in anticipation of your offspring's graduation. *Smart Tip:* Your best time to list the property for sale is in advance of the demand cycle that rises from the university's housing placement schedule. In the event the property doesn't sell immediately, the listing will be active during the peak season for housing. On the flip side, the best time to avoid is the off-season between July and October when student housing has the least demand.

It bears repeating that value in college-town real estate is generated in a number of ways. You get cash from monthly rents. You get tax savings from depreciation and other deductions, which you can put in your pocket year-round by adjusting your tax withholding. You'll have long-term appreciation going for you when you buy smart. You'll see equity buildup from loan pay-down. Plus, when you invest your cash flow — or pay down an equity loan — you'll see growth in your other investments and your cash too.

There will come a time when you've built up enough equity in a college property that you decide you want to put that equity to work. Idle equity in a property means resources going unused. Knowing when to cash out from an investment is essential. Do it right and you'll have cash in hand for other investments or expenses or to use as a down payment on more rental properties. Remember the *Essential Takeaway* from your ORIENTATION in Chapter 1: A larger number of less expensive properties is better than a few more costly ones.

| **Timing Your Moment To Cash Out** | One trick to riding the highs and lows of college-town markets is to keep an eye on local supply and demand indicators. In your crystal ball, watch what existing home sales are doing along with trends in new-home building |

permits, university housing projects, mortgage defaults, foreclosures and interest rates so you can buy on the low end of a cycle and sell near the top. Here are the four phases of every real estate cycle:

1. **Development:** Builders build to meet a demand. This is a good time to sell.

2. **Overbuilding:** The local economy slows down. Demand drops, but builders complete construction underway.

3. **Adjustment:** Developers and lenders curtail new construction starts.

4. **Acquisition:** The economy picks up. Buyers start shopping again. This is a good time to buy, while prices are down and sellers are anxious to sell.

Watch university enrollment rates. Enrollments trending down mean the student housing resale market will also be trending down. Watch the local housing market. Lower inventories and rising prices that reflect a seller's market mean it's a smart time to sell. Watch the rental market. When vacancy rates are falling and rents are rising, other investors will pay top dollar for your property.

Most important: Take your own pulse as an investor. Kids graduate. Times change. Portfolios change. Income needs change. The essential time to cash in your investment is when you are ready—regardless of the market. One smart technique to know when the time is right is an "equity target" strategy.

**Recognize
How Equity
Buildup Triggers
Profit-Taking**

Equity buildup — the difference between the property value and the outstanding loan balance — triggers the right time to profit from your investment real estate. For example: When a $100,000 property that was purchased with $10,000 down and financed by a $90,000 loan, reaches $120,000 in value, equity is $30,000 ($120,000 less $90,000 = $30,000). (To keep things simple, we've left out the equity increase from monthly principal payoffs that also increase your equity.)

Some investors call equity buildup "shadow income" because it is not realized until the investor takes the profit through refinancing or selling. Some smart investors set an "equity target" when write-offs from depreciation have run out — or the ratio of principal to interest payments no longer provides large mortgage interest deductions. Both stages dramatically reduce your leverage. In our example, the $100,000 property bought with $10,000 down means a loan-to-value (LTV) ratio of 90% ($90,000 divided by $100,000 = 90% LTV). Equity increases as the property appreciates until loan-to-value, in our example, becomes 75% ($90,000 divided by $120,000 = 75% LTV). Translated into leverage lingo, your equity (leverage) has increased from 10% to 25%. Bingo. You've hit your 25% equity target, and it's time to take profits from equity. (As before, with principal pay-down you may reach a larger equity target even faster than this example.)

◆ ◆ ◆

Essential Takeaway: *Appreciation can go on forever, literally. That's why some "hold" investors advise against ever selling a property. Why? Even after removing cash with an equity loan or cash-out refinancing, your investment continues to grow more valuable as its potential sale price goes up. Smart investors know you can continue to realize appreciation gains even while transferring cash into new investments. Quite simply: Take out built-up equity, buy another property, hold it, repeat. That's how hold investors get rich slowly with college-town real estate.*

◆ ◆ ◆

78

GRADUATION

5 SMART STRATEGIES TO TAKE YOUR MONEY AND RUN

🗩 Strategy #1: Sell Property

Understand that rental markets don't always cooperate. Perhaps lenders won't refinance your property at an acceptably high loan-to-value, or the appraisal of market value is so low that refinancing is not a reasonable alternative, or you need the cash fast for an unexpected reason. Selling the property is the answer to take out maximum equity profits. Before you decide, you'll want to factor in selling expenses from brokerage fees, fix-up expenses, seller-paid discount points and maybe vacancy in the transition.

Ask your investment real estate agent and accountant if selling expenses in your situation fit within the general rule of 8%-10% of sale price. Remember: Your profits from sale will be taxed at lower capital gains rates if property was held for more than a year. Plus, you want to be sure to factor in adjustments for recapture of excess depreciation, which will add income (profit) to your taxable personal income (see example following).

Word to the wise: Serious sellers in search of serious buyers—not just tire kickers—work with their real estate agent and consider adding these requests in the "agent notes" section of the listing.

Seller requests the following:

▶ All buyers be pre-approved prior to viewing property.
▶ Pre-approval letter must accompany offer (if an all-cash sale, then proof of funds required before seller's written acceptance of any contract).
▶ Earnest-money deposit of not less than 1.5% of asking price (pick your percentage).

Crunch your numbers to estimate net proceeds from sale before you list. Smart investors take their calculations a step further by figuring the net proceeds of sale after taxes. Basically, you subtract the costs of selling, mortgage balance, and any tax liability from the sale price to come up with a "net walk-away cash" figure. The calculations look like this:

▶ Sale price: $120,000
Less:
▶ Costs of selling: $12,000

▶ Mortgage balance: $90,000

Proceeds Sub-total: $18,000

Less:

▶ Tax liability†: $8,166

Net proceeds of sale after taxes: $9,833 ($18,000 – $8,166 = $9,833)

> †† *Tax Liability*
> Tax liability is calculated in our example to be based on $29,166 taxable income x 28% marginal tax bracket = $8,166. The $29,166 taxable income figure ("recapture") comes from subtracting the allowed straight-line depreciation from the years of actual accelerated depreciation claimed ($68,055 accelerated less $38,889 straight-line = $29,166 taxable income). Again, these hypothetical figures are for illustration only.

Get on the radar screen of motivated buyers. Many college markets are truly small towns. Getting the word out about your sale can be very straightforward:

> ▶ Mail a letter to absentee non-occupant owner/investors found in the tax records or the landlords association.
>
> ▶ Advertise "Property for Sale" in the student newspaper or online equivalent.
>
> ▶ Run an ad in the rental classifieds section: "Rather buy than rent?" is a grabber headline.
>
> ▶ Mail or email "Why pay another landlord's mortgage?" letter with property flyer to the home mailing list of last year's incoming students, if available from the housing office.
>
> ▶ Spread word through the community of property managers, real estate agents and lender professionals that work with college-rental clients.
>
> ▶ Craigslist.
>
> ▶ Building or unit signage.
>
> ▶ Mentor, partner, other local investors.
>
> ▶ Staff and faculty intranets or other associations/groups.
>
> ▶ Property management companies—some own properties and may consider adding yours to their portfolio.

Expand your buyer pool beyond the investor community.
Beyond the normal steady stream of buyers from parents and investors coming out of more-affluent urban communities, you'll also discover retirees — especially former academicians — and professionals flock to college towns for the culture, lifestyle, libraries and access to health care. Some universities are even building facilities to attract their retired alumni. For retirees, managing a property while living in a unit or nearby can be an attractive part-time occupation. *Smart Tip:* Keep this option in mind when you originally buy a small multi-unit property. College-town retirees make reliable property managers or may be your ultimate buyer when you want to sell. Or, if you're shopping for a single-family property, consider carefully that your college student's idea of a perfect place to live off campus may not match your idea of a great place to retire.

● Strategy #2: Installment Sale To Defer Taxes
Instead of taking the proceeds as a lump sum, some investors take back their equity in the form of a second or third mortgage to the purchaser. In today's market with more renters who lost their homes to foreclosure, getting financing from their landlord (also, "rent-to-buy," "lease-purchase"), rather than a lender, can be very attractive to some tenants. Essentially, you receive the equity over a period of time as installment payments plus interest, rather than one big check at settlement. You can structure the deal many ways. One example: A written contract gives tenant an option to buy the property at an agreed-upon price after an agreed-upon number of years. There may be an option-to-buy fee that can range from several hundred dollars to several thousand (say, 5% of home's value). An extra amount may be added to rent payments that can be applied to the future down payment or purchase price.

Why do this? The largest benefit of an installment sale, besides receiving current income just like you enjoyed from rent, is being able to defer your profits — and thus defer capital gains taxes. Remember, tax rules require you to declare in the year of sale all depreciation for recapture. If you have an installment sale, you only have to report each installment payment that is a percentage of the remaining profit from the entire sale. Essentially, you pay capital gains on the installment payments, not the entire sale price. Sound complicated? Not really, but it takes some planning. Be sure to consult your tax advisor to weigh the implications in your situation.

● Strategy #3: Equity Loan or HELOC Payoff

One option is to borrow against the equity in the property by using an equity loan or home equity line of credit (HELOC), which is a second or third mortgage on the property. This cash can become the foundation for an expansion of your real estate investments. *Smart Tip:* Smart investors who used an outside equity loan, perhaps on their own residence, for their investment down payment, use positive cash flow to pay down that original equity loan gradually until the day the renewed credit gives them available cash to invest in another property using the original credit line or loan. Although this strategy does not take out an equity loan on the investment property per se, the cash outcome is the same. This payoff strategy works especially well when cash flow is healthy.

● Strategy #4: Cash-Out Refinancing

With the refinancing strategy, you keep the property, but simply increase your leverage with a new tax-free loan. Talk with your trusted lender to determine if it is best to refinance the entire first trust or obtain a commercial second-trust mortgage for a portion of the equity (Strategy #3). Either way, the new loan puts cash in your pocket tax-free (until sale later). You can use the cash for other purposes, improve the property to maintain value or increase rental income. Or, as many investors do, you can reinvest the cash into a down payment on another property that suits your goals. That last move requires no additional outlay beyond the proceeds realized from refinancing. Smart.

- ▶ New market value: $120,000
- ▶ Old loan balance: $90,000
- ▶ Equity available for refinancing: $30,000 (less LTV requirements of lender)

A secondary benefit of this strategy is that refinancing gives you increased mortgage interest deductions that can offset higher rental income generated by improvements or simply higher rents over the years.

● Strategy #5: Defer Taxes With A 1031 Exchange

Rather than pay taxes on profits from the sale of an income-producing property, you can defer taxation by exchanging a qualified property for another "like-kind" property. It's called a 1031 exchange (also, "tax-deferred exchange"), named after Internal Revenue Code (IRC) section 1031.

Here are the essentials involved in a tax-deferred property exchange. *Smart Tip:* Due to the complexities and possible tax consequences of this type of transaction, be sure to consult a tax professional and/or a real estate attorney before attempting to execute a 1031 exchange.

What types of property can be exchanged? Real estate qualified for a tax-deferred exchange includes improved or unimproved property held for income, investment or business purposes. Both the old ("relinquished") property and the new ("replacement") property would have to fall within that definition for the transaction to be a qualified "like-kind" exchange.

You could, for example, exchange unimproved land for an improved property you intend to use as an investment or for your business—but not as your residence. Or, you could exchange ownership of one qualified property for ownership of multiple like-kind properties—and vice versa. A number of possibilities are available as are a variety of limitations.

Can I take some money out of the transaction by investing in a property of lower value? To have a valid tax-deferred exchange, you must exchange the old property for a property of equal or greater value. If at the conclusion of the transaction you receive any cash, cash equivalents or non-like-kind property, you will owe capital gains taxes.

Also note, a 1031 exchange only defers taxation until such time as you sell the replacement property and take the money.

Can I simply sell one property and buy another in a 1031 exchange? No. To reap the tax break, there must be an exchange, not just a sale and purchase of otherwise qualified properties. The exchange must be properly executed through an exchange agreement serviced by a "qualified intermediary" according to a specific process and timetable defined by the tax code.

What is a qualified intermediary? Sometimes called a "facilitator" or "accommodator," a qualified intermediary (QI) functions as a middleman between you (the exchangor) and the buyers and sellers of the properties involved. Because you are not allowed to take physical possession or "constructive receipt" of the proceeds of the sale of your old property, the QI holds all the cash from the exchange until it is transferred to the seller of the replacement property. The QI facilitates the acquisition and transfer of the properties, providing documentation to ensure the exchange meets tax-code requirements. Your "exchange agreement" with the QI limits access to proceeds during the exchange, and may stipulate other services provided for an agreed-upon fee.

A QI must be an independent third party to the exchange. Neither you, your buyer or seller can serve as a QI in your exchange, nor can anyone who in the previous two years has been your employee, attorney, accountant, investment broker, real estate agent/broker or relative.

Be aware, there are no licensing requirements for QIs, and the industry is largely unregulated. Because the QI is entrusted to hold all the funds involved in your 1031 exchange, it is important you select one that is reputable, experienced, financially sound and bonded.

Is there more than one way to structure a 1031 exchange?

There are two basic types of real property exchanges, each conducted according to timetables and rules outlined by Internal Revenue Code (IRC) and Treasury regulations.

1. Simultaneous Exchange: This occurs when both your old property and your new property go to closing (or settlement) on the same day.

2. Delayed Exchange: Settlement is non-simultaneous, with closing on the old property occurring on a different day and before closing on the replacement property. With delayed exchanges, strict timing requirements must be adhered to. You must close on or formally identify a replacement property within 45 calendar days of closing on the old property. In addition, you must close on the identified replacement property by one of two deadlines, whichever is earlier:

▶ Within 180 calendar days of the transfer of the old property; or,

▶ By the due date of the income tax return for the tax year during which the old property was closed.

A number of other requirements apply to the delayed exchange process. Be sure to discuss them with your tax and legal advisors.

Parking Arrangements

There are two types of "parking" arrangements:

1. Reverse Exchange: Your replacement property is closed before you find a buyer for your relinquished property.

2. Improvement Exchange: You make improvements to a new or existing replacement property, investing the exchange proceeds.

Under the "safe harbor" rules, you must complete these non-simultaneous exchanges within 180 calendar days of title transfer to an "exchange accommodation titleholder" (generally a separate entity, such as an LLC owned by the QI), and you must identify the property to be relinquished within 45 calendar days. Again, consult your qualified tax and legal advisors for all the details relating to reverse and improvement exchanges.

Don't expect to use your real estate agent to conduct a 1031 exchange. A real estate professional who has served you professionally within the two years prior to the exchange agreement is disqualified from serving as the QI in your 1031 exchange. Where your agent can be invaluable is in helping you identify buyers for the property you want to sell and in helping you locate qualified like-kind replacement property.

Especially if you are considering a delayed or reverse exchange, you'll want to have an experienced, well-networked real estate professional on your side helping you meet the 45-day identification and 180-day exchange period deadlines. Knowing how 1031 exchanges work, your agent must be dedicated to ensuring that the sale and purchase of your investment properties come off smoothly — and tax-deferred!

CONGRATULATIONS!

In many areas of the country, as we said in the beginning, college-town real estate is experiencing a convergence of lower prices, high inventory, low interest rates and higher rents. The housing crash turned millions of homeowners and new households into renters. The tide of Echo Boomers — and others — headed to university in the coming years guarantees demand.

There you have it.

Today is one of the best times in a generation to buy college-town real estate, no matter if it's single family homes, townhomes or condos.

The stunning fact is crystal clear: *Get rich slowly* strategies are paying off handsomely in this market.

So, maybe it's the perfect time to grow your own real estate investing portfolio. Keep in mind our cardinal rule: It's better to own several less expensive student rentals than one expensive property. When you do invest in your next college rental, you'll be even smarter.

If you know someone who is planning to invest soon, pay it forward by recommending SMART ESSENTIALS FOR COLLEGE RENTALS.

Congratulations again, Smartie!

Chapter 7 Roundup

Smart Essentials GRADUATION ::
What You Have Learned

▶▶ Smart ways to time your market exit.
▶▶ Recognize how equity buildup triggers profit taking.
▶▶ 5 smart strategies to take your money and run.
　▶ *Strategy #1:* Sell property.
　▶ *Strategy #2:* Installment sale to defer taxes.
　▶ *Strategy #3:* Equity loan or HELOC payoff.
　▶ *Strategy #4:* Cash-out refinancing.
　▶ *Strategy #5:* Defer taxes with a 1031 exchange.

Smart Essentials

Page	Essential Note

About The Series

SMART ESSENTIALS was written for you.

We know because you tell us. Our readers are smart, busy, capable people stressed by the fact that they only get one chance to get it right buying or selling real estate. You tell us on our *http://www.SmartEssentials.com* website and in your emails. You appreciate smart, useful, distilled information that goes straight to the point.

Certainly, our readers *can* swim through the tides of endless online articles searching for useful information. Certainly, our readers *can* slog through full length how-to books trying to glean the chapter here or there that they really need hidden in the general filler. But you're too smart for that. You appreciate concise ideas that can make you tens of thousands in profit when you sell real estate and save you thousands at the settlement table when you buy — or avoid costly mistakes you didn't have to make.

You want the information now. You want it smartly presented. You want it current for today's market. Mostly you want your information concise, concentrated and applicable to your situation.

● Like the stressed-out bride who thanked us for advising that soon-to-be-newlyweds start looking for a home three months *after* the wedding.

● Like the Canadian investor who appreciated learning that California charges a transfer tax on non-resident sales, so he bought in Nevada.

● Like the thankful divorced Dad who bought two extra bedrooms for sleepovers on custody weekends.

● And like the thankful parents who saved thousands over seven years (two serial college kids) by investing in rentable student housing because at their state university most students had to rent off-campus housing.

We also know most of our readers typically buy multiple SMART ESSENTIALS. Not only because most sellers are buyers and most buyers become sellers, but mostly because you have smart friends. You talk. Naturally. After all, you just spent the last few months consumed by one of the largest life-shaping transactions of your life. Who wouldn't need to vent?

That's why we wrote every SMART ESSENTIALS for you.

Let us know what you think. More important, when you run across one of those incredible little nuggets of street-smart wisdom during your transaction, email us or share it as a Smarties' Story on our website. We love your stories. And the thousands of other Smarties facing the same situation will thank you, too. Giving is sharing. And sharing is the best way we know to enhance love.

Looking forward to hearing from you!

Dan Gooder Richard
Series Editor

Dan Gooder Richard can be contacted at:

SMART ESSENTIALS
c/o Inkspiration Media
2724 Dorr Avenue, Suite 103
Fairfax, VA 22031
(703) 698-7750
CollegeRentals@SmartEssentials.com
http://www.SmartEssentials.com

About The Team

A venture the size of SMART ESSENTIALS requires an outstanding team. Dan Gooder Richard is the editor of SMART ESSENTIALS and author of COLLEGE RENTALS. Dan's first book, *REAL ESTATE RAINMAKER®: Successful Strategies for Real Estate Marketing,* was published by John Wiley & Sons in 2000. Dan's second book, *REAL ESTATE RAINMAKER®: Guide to Online Marketing,* was published by John Wiley & Sons in 2004. He is also creator of the RAINMAKER LEAD SYSTEM® now in use by thousands of real estate professionals nationwide. He and his wife, Synnove Granholm, founded GOODER GROUP® in 1983 and continue to manage the Fairfax, Virginia-based publisher of marketing materials for real estate and mortgage professionals. Hats off to Deborah Rhoney, our managing editor and principal writer. She puts the smart into the essentials. Amy Hausman, our marketing diva and writer, keeps the buzz going with every new publication. Special thanks to our web master, Tammy Waitsman, and our social media guru, Jesse Hickman, for making the online side of SMART ESSENTIALS truly click. Jane Rooney, our controller at Inkspiration Media, keeps us on track and on forecast. Stephanie Simmons keeps the service to readers stellar and makes the smallest detail her mission. A special thanks to David Wu, of DW Design, whose branding and graphic design makes us all look good. To the entire team at SMART ESSENTIALS—thank you—we couldn't do it without you!

SMARTIES' CREED

🔊 **I will express my voice** at *http://www.SmartEssentials.com* and become part of the world's smartest communities.

🔊 **I will help others get smarter for less.** I simply share with two. And they tell two. If we pay it forward 33 times, we can reach every person in the world.

🔊 **I will keep up to date** and with one click, one post, one random act of selflessness, I will be smarter, happier, richer.

🔊 **I can imagine** where everyone reading my voice did something today to improve others. The world would be a smarter place . . . and it all would be thanks to my original, selfless act to help others.

SMART TALK

The fact that you are reading this sentence tells us a lot about you. Clearly, you have a hunger for wisdom to increase your college-town real estate smarts. Having gotten this far, it's likely you've got insights, experiences and questions of your own to share. Now it's time to reach out to other Smarties by sharing your answers and questions at the Smart Talk knowledge center: http://www.SmartEssentials.com. *We'll all be smarter for it!*

Pay it forward at *http://www.SmartEssentials.com* today!

More Titles In Best-Selling SMART ESSENTIALS Series

🔊 SMART ESSENTIALS FOR SELLING YOUR HOME
How To Get The Highest Price In The Shortest Time

🔊 SMART ESSENTIALS FOR BUYING A HOME
How To Get The Best Price And The Lowest Payment

🔊 SMART ESSENTIALS FOR REAL ESTATE INVESTING
How To Build Wealth In Rental Property Today

🔊 SMART ESSENTIALS FOR BUYING FORECLOSURES
Finding Hidden Bargains For Home Or Profit

🔊 SMART ESSENTIALS FOR COLLEGE RENTALS
Parent and Investor Guide To Buying College-Town Real Estate

Made in the USA
San Bernardino, CA
28 October 2015